LIFE ISN'T ABOUT WAITING FOR THE STORM TO PASS.
IT'S ABOUT LEARNING TO DANCE IN THE RAIN!

REACHING BEYOND THE CLOUDS

From Undiagnosed to Climbing Mt. Everest

CINDY L. ABBOTT

Editor Stacie Parra

Photo Editor Eric Hanauer

Cover Photo by Bill Allen, Mountain Trip International

Back Cover Author Photo by Ania Lichota

Reaching Beyond the Clouds www.reachingbeyondtheclouds.com

ISBN: 0615482910
ISBN-13: 9780615482910
Library of Congress Control Number: 2011928497
Cindy L. Abbott

With love to

my husband, Larry

and

my daughter, Teshia.

All of our stories and experiences are unique

and

this is mine.

CONTENTS

Chapter 1

SOMETHING IS WRONG

April 1, 2010

Speechless and crying I forced myself out of my husband's arms and stepped across the thick, black tape of the airport security line. I did not look back. I couldn't. If I did, I might change my mind. With tears running down my cheeks, I walked away from the man I loved, the only life I knew, and headed toward the unknown.

As I continued through the chained pathway toward the x-ray screening station, I knew something was wrong. It felt as if that black tape on the airport floor had somehow changed me. The feeling was immediate and with each step, it grew more intense, but it wasn't sadness or fear. Yes, I was leaving my family, my home, everything familiar behind, but that wasn't it. I couldn't shake this unexplainable sense that something was wrong. The kind of wrong that nearly caused me to turn around and go home. But I didn't. I just stepped into the security screening line.

Waiting in line with sandals in hand, I noticed the bright orange-striped socks of the shoeless man standing in front of me. I couldn't resist. I said, "Hello, I like your socks." And that began a wonderfully insightful and fun conversation with David, an art dealer. Turns out, David was not only on the same flight, he was also seated directly behind me. During our 15 hours in the air we talked about many things – our families, travel adventures, and the fact that we both had serious rare diseases. This unlikely meeting turned into a great distraction, which finally allowed me to relax, even sleep.

After a short nap, I began writing a journal of my experiences and thoughts, which I planned to give to my husband, Larry when I returned home.

My first entry:

April 2nd

So, as I sit on the plane halfway through the flight to Hong Kong, I am already doubting my ability to be away from Larry so long. It's as if a part of me is not here – I must have forgotten to pack my heart. But it's safe with him at home ☺. I find comfort that he is in our bed with our cats, and hope that he can tell that my heart is with him. He is me! We are one! Perfect love!

And suddenly, mystery solved! That terrible feeling of wrongness that had been plaguing me since the security line, the overwhelming feeling that nearly made me turn around before I stepped foot on the plane, was actually emptiness. I think as I walked the security line at the airport I must have subconsciously realized that my husband and I were now divided – at that time by the line of black tape on the airport floor, but soon it would be by far more – continents, mountains, months. In our 25 years together, we'd never been apart for more than a few days. I wondered how, and if, I'd be able to cope with this long separation.

We landed in Hong Kong, and before departing the plane, David wished me a safe journey and then gave me a 3,000-year old Dzi stone bead. He said it would bring positive energy to the person wearing it. I put it on immediately. His gift surprised and touched me, and this single act of kindness and caring would be the first of many I'd experience over the course of the coming months.

My journey to Mt. Everest began three years ago but my story, like so many other victims of rare, unknown diseases, started more than a decade earlier. Around 1994 I began to experience a variety of unusual physical problems: loss of vision, extreme fatigue, shooting pain in my legs, sinus problems, and headaches. Thirteen years and countless medical exams and tests later, the cause of my symptoms remained a mystery. It was terrifying to have serious health issues that doctors couldn't explain. They simply had no idea what was causing these problems and could offer me no advice, much less diagnosis. As the symptoms intensified, I became desperate to find someone or something that could help.

Of the many problems I was experiencing, the one that concerned me the most was my rapidly deteriorating vision. At the rate I was losing sight, I estimated I'd be blind in 6 months! I believe that I can handle just about anything, but the thought of going blind terrified me. I set aside my other physical problems, and focused on saving my vision.

By this time however, I had already seen many eye doctors, none of whom had any idea why I was losing my vision. They couldn't stop it; they couldn't even slow it down. I'd go to one doctor who'd refer me to another doctor who would refer me to yet another doctor. Not one of them helped. Then it hit me. I was responsible for me and I had to take control of the situation or go blind.

Years earlier I had overheard a conversation about the Jules Stein Eye Institute at UCLA, so I called the main number and scheduled an appointment. I had to complete the necessary paperwork before seeing the doctor, and when I came to the line "Referred by," it was an amazingly powerful feeling to write in "myself." From now on I was going to be actively involved, and for the most part, in control of and responsible for my own medical care.

Enter Dr. Gary Holland of the Jules Stein Eye Institute, an amazing doctor who worked tirelessly to save my deteriorating vision. Dr. Holland diagnosed me with retinal vasculitis (inflammation of the blood vessels in the eye). And while there was still no answer as to "why" this was happening, at least I now had some hope of saving my sight. Consequently, I began a treatment program that dramatically slowed my vision loss. Unfortunately, one of the side effects of the treatment is eye damage, and I'd eventually have to make a tough choice: stop treatment and resume rapid vision loss or continue treatment and suffer vision loss as a side effect of the treatment. I would make that decision when the time came.

———

My health issues have never slowed me down. My husband and I love to explore the world. Each year we use the money in our travel fund to embark on some wild adventure. We plan and we save and we follow our dreams. Larry has made a list of the places we want to explore, and I believe it'll keep us criss-crossing the globe for the next 15 years or so. We're not wealthy, but adventure travel is a priority in our lives, and our children encourage us along our path. We'll never wake up one day and ask, "Where did life go?"

Larry often pulls out the list and the world atlas, and we spread out on our bed and begin plotting where and when we'll go next. First, we look at each item on the list to see if any can be combined into one trip. Many times Larry picks one part of the trip and I pick another. It may take three or four years of saving both money and airline miles, but eventually we're on our way. We've been SCUBA diving with whale sharks in the Galapagos Islands, walked miles along the Great Wall of China, seen polar bears in the wilds of northern Alaska, and zip-lined through the Costa Rican jungle.

A lot of our trip research and inspiration comes through television documentaries. For example, we saw a program about the pink dolphins that inhabit the Amazon River. Three years later, we were swimming in the Amazon alongside those dolphins. Next, we saw a nature show about a four-week old cheetah cub in a South African Animal Reserve. Four years after that, we were petting that cheetah named Kane.

Nice kitty-kitty!

In the Spring of 2007, we watched an amazing Discovery Channel show called *Everest: Beyond the Limit*. At the end of the miniseries, I turned to my husband and said, "I have to climb Mt. Everest." Knowing me better than I think I know myself, Larry realized I was serious and I believe his reply at the time was something like, "Are you crazy!?!" "Why not?" I answered. The trek to Mt. Everest Base Camp had been on our list for many years. Base Camp was one thing, but at the age of 62, Larry knew his limits and had no intention of attempting to summit the world's tallest mountain. I, on the other hand, felt drawn to climb Everest. I'm not sure if it was the beauty, the challenge, maybe both, but I had to do it. The fact that I knew almost nothing about mountain climbing did not deter me. I'd learn.

To me, climbing Mt. Everest didn't seem impossible, but what did I know? The year before, Larry and I summited Mt. Kilimanjaro, the highest mountain in Africa standing at 19,334 feet above sea level. Mt. Kilimanjaro was not a technical climb, but its height and terrain gave us an idea of what it was like, both mentally and physically, to climb a big mountain. However, our Kilimanjaro climb was fully supported, meaning we hiked carrying light day-packs, didn't have to set up camp, and had all our meals prepared for us. Yes, I had been up one big mountain, but I was certainly no mountaineer; not even close.

Many people climb for years or even decades before taking on the challenge of a mountain like Everest. There are countless factors to consider: technical climbing skills; the effects of extreme altitude; the ability to read and predict snow, ice, and weather conditions; physical and mental strength; money; and time away from work, home, and family. The list is endless. To a rational person, what I was proposing would seem impossible, even crazy, but not to me.

So, at the age of 48, I was about to start training for a new adventure – mountain climbing. My first step was to find a guide willing to take on the challenge, and after doing some research, I found Scott Woolums, a very experienced high-altitude guide who was a three-time Everest summiter. I called him one afternoon in the spring of 2007. I introduced myself and said, "I want to climb Mt. Everest." There was dead silence on the other end of the line, and then Scott finally replied, "Well, we do not start by climbing Mt. Everest." We had a great conversation. Scott was professional yet personable, and I really liked the way he handled my request. We made arrangements to climb Mt. Aconcagua in Argentina (the highest mountain in South America). And just like that, Larry and I were scheduled to leave in December for my first Mt. Everest training climb. Then it happened!

Chapter 2

THE ANSWER: A LIFE CHANGING EVENT OR WAS IT?

On June 8, 2007, while shopping at a local gardening store I was overcome with vertigo and nausea, and I was having trouble walking. Then I realized I could not see out of one eye. I didn't understand. Only the day before I had seen Dr. Holland at Jules Stein Eye Institute for my eight-week check-up and he had found nothing unusual. Somehow I had to get myself home, so I got in the car and slowly made my way the few miles back to the house. I called Dr. Holland's office, but he wasn't in. So I talked with one of the resident doctors who told me to come in immediately. It was now late afternoon on a Friday. In rush-hour traffic, it would take hours to drive to Los Angeles, and by the time I got there, the medical offices would certainly be closed. My vision was also so disorienting that there was no way I could drive myself to UCLA. After explaining all of that to the resident doctor, he suggested that I go to a local emergency hospital. I said that was pointless because I knew the drill: they'd order a bunch of tests, keep me for hours, have no idea what happened or how to treat me, and then send me home. So the resident doctor acquiesced and made me an appointment to see Dr. Holland first thing Monday morning.

Dr. Holland had been treating my retinal vasculitis for years. During that time I had seen many emergency patients come into his office, and now I was one of them. After taking one look inside my eye, he ordered a test called a fluorescein retinal angiogram. This test used a special camera to take a series of pictures that showed the blood vessels inside the eye. The angiogram test had been part of my regular eye exams for years, so I was familiar with how my blood vessels should look. After the angiogram, the technician handed me the pictures to take downstairs to Dr. Holland. While in the elevator, I examined them and was shocked by what I saw. It looked as if a blood bomb had exploded inside my left eye! Many of the blood vessels were completely destroyed, and isolated pockets of blood were scattered throughout the clear, jelly-like fluid of my inner eye. Imagine taking a paint brush, dipping it in red paint, and then flinging the paint onto a white dinner plate. That's what it looked like; the blood bursts were the shrapnel of the bomb that had gone off in my eye.

As I walked toward Dr. Holland's office, focused on the pictures the whole time, my reaction turned from shock to fear to obscure fascination. In an odd way, the images resembled pieces of abstract art. I started wondering what would cause this to happen. That's how I deal with stressful situations; I turn them into learning opportunities, and this was no different. In that moment, I changed from patient to investigator. It was time to collect data and analyze the situation. It was the only way I would be able to make an educated, non-emotional decision about my worsening medical condition, and prevent myself from going into total shock.

Dr. Holland came into the examination room, and I handed him the pictures and said, "They look cool but I don't think that's good." And it wasn't. I had suffered a central retinal vein occlusion. A blood vessel near the optic nerve had burst. Dr. Holland could tell me what had happened but not why. So he asked his colleague, Dr. Kreiger, and a resident, Dr. Cappelle, to have a look. They all agreed that I'd suffered a vascular occlusion, but again, no one could explain why.

While the doctors conferred, I began to do some analysis of my own. Isn't what happened to my eye similar to what happens when blood vessels break under the skin? The blood pools and turns into a bruise, and within a few days the body removes the blood, and the bruise disappears. So, under that rationale, wouldn't my body just remove the blood from my inner eye, and then my vision would return? It had been three days since it'd happened, and I could already see a little bit better. So, in a hopeful voice, I asked the doctors how long it would be until my vision in my left eye completely returned. Their response was kind but honest – they didn't know if it ever would.

I returned to Dr. Holland's office three days later hoping for news that my eye was clearing up. But it wasn't. While the blood bursts were dissipating, it turns out that they were not the cause of the vision loss. The problem was actually the blood vessels *around* the optic nerve. They were permanently damaged; one minute I'm walking around a gardening shop, and the next, I'm functionally blind in my left eye.

As I sat in the examination room chair waiting for the doctors to return, I felt sad and mad. The cause of my retinal vasculitis, and the subsequent occlusion, needed an answer. I knew that it was a chronic condition, and that if it wasn't stopped, would leave me completely blind. And if that happened, how would I adjust? How would I be able to keep working as a teacher and income tax preparer? How would I manage my home and care for my family? What would I do if I had to give up my hobbies of adventure traveling and underwater videography? If we didn't figure out what this was and stop it, my life would be forever changed. I needed some answers. What was taking the doctors so long?

Dr. Holland and Dr. Kreiger finally returned but not with answers, only more questions. They found something in my medical history, that when combined with my recent vascular occlusion, triggered a suspicion, a hunch, and they told me to see a rheumatologist for more tests. Before I left their office, I asked Dr. Holland if they performed eye transplants. I joked that eye color didn't matter; I'd take anything! I just needed a new eye. He smiled at me, but didn't answer. Dr. Holland had become accustomed to my sense of humor. He understood that it was my way of dealing with the reality of the sad news.

I went back to see Dr. Holland and Dr. Kreiger on Monday, June 18th, just four days after the bad transplant joke. And after a brief eye exam, I walked across the street to Ronald Reagan Medical Center to see the rheumatologist they had recommended, Dr. Alan Gorn. His waiting room was filled with seriously ill people. Many of them had walkers or wheel chairs, and were wearing nose pieces or face masks hooked up to portable oxygen tanks. And there I was, 48-years old and the picture of health on the outside. I felt out of place. I kept thinking, "I'm not like them. I just have a vision problem." These people were very sick and I felt guilty for being there and taking up the doctor's valuable time. I sat back in a corner, out of view, while I waited.

Dr. Gorn was running behind schedule, but judging by the people I observed in the waiting room, I understood why he was late, and patiently waited my turn. When Dr. Gorn finally walked into the exam room, he introduced himself, shook my hand, and apologized for the delay. Like the doctors at the eye institute, I immediately felt comfortable with Dr. Gorn, and despite being extremely busy and far behind schedule, he sat down and gave me his full attention. He began by questioning me about my past medical problems, not just the recent issue with my vision. I told him about everything: the blood in the urine, the sinus surgery, the joint pain, the extreme fatigue, and the misdiagnosis of multiple sclerosis. For the first time in 13 years, a doctor was collecting my entire medical history in order to put together the complex, detailed picture. But could he make sense of enough of the pieces to form a recognizable image, an actual diagnosis?

Dr. Gorn completed his initial exam and ordered more x-rays and laboratory tests. I spent the next few hours going from department to department at UCLA. It wasn't until I was in the car for the two-hour drive home that I had time to think. I can't say that I felt hopeful, I knew better. But, I did feel relief. It seemed like Dr. Gorn might actually be able to find the missing pieces needed to solve the mystery of the medical condition that had plagued me for so long.

I had an appointment with Dr. Gorn to go over the test results the following Thursday. Again I found myself sitting in that waiting room with all those sick people, and as I sat there, I thought back on the last 13 years: all the doctors, all the tests, and all the times I waited, just like now, only to be told that they didn't know and couldn't help. I had become numb to the process. There was no anxiety or fear; I just waited.

Dr. Gorn entered the room with my chart in hand, and sat down. It was only our second meeting, but I had an idea of what he dealt with on a daily basis, simply by what I saw in his waiting room. I pictured him going from one room to another, closing one door and leaving behind that patient and concern, taking three steps, opening the next door to the next patient and concern. In this case, it was me.

I always sat in the chair in the exam rooms, never on the exam table itself. There was no need for the table. I knew what I had wasn't something that could be seen or felt. And besides, I had to sit close to the doctor so we could read the reports together. I was conducting an investigation and needed to understand the facts. With pencil in hand, I was ready.

Dr. Gorn went over the test results. For the most part, he told me what I didn't have: not lupus, not HIV, not MS. He used the process of elimination initially to narrow down the field. Now that he knew what I didn't have, he could order more specific tests. So I went back to the lab. This time the phlebotomist drew so many tubes of blood, I was surprised that I didn't faint on the way out of the room. Again, I had to wait for the lab results but this time there was a complication.

Earlier in the week I had mentioned to both Dr. Gorn and Dr. Holland that my husband and I were scheduled to leave that Sunday for a four-week diving vacation to Indonesia. While my vision was not improving, it was also not getting worse, and the tests had not revealed anything new. We'd been planning this trip for two years. It was paid for and I wanted to go. Both of the doctors were surprised that I would consider leaving the country to go diving in Indonesia in my condition. But what was *my* condition? And, neither of them could give me a valid reason why I couldn't or shouldn't go. From my perspective, I had been traveling and diving for years with whatever I had, and except for my decreased vision, nothing else had changed.

———

Larry and I left for our month-long diving vacation three days after my last appointment with Dr. Gorn. But before we went, I promised Larry, the doctors, and myself that if anything happened I would catch the first flight home. Was I taking a risk by going? Sure. But I wasn't ready to stop living life, not yet anyway.

This was our third trip to Indonesia. On our previous visits, we had explored Bali, Raja Ampat, and the Flores Sea, including Komodo Island (the home of the mighty Komodo dragons). This time, we were headed to Sulawesi and the Lembeh Strait for muck diving, but our first stop was the remote island of Kri in Raja Ampat, one of my favorite dive locations.

The days turned into weeks as we traveled across Indonesia. Although I had some difficulty adjusting to diving with my limited vision, I didn't notice anything else unusual. But to be on the safe side, I made conservative dives and skipped some altogether in order to take naps, relax, or read. I consciously tried not to stress my body. Indonesia was no place to have a medical emergency.

We spent the last week of our vacation on a live-aboard dive boat. It's like a tiny cruise ship for divers. It was there that I noticed that when I bumped into something I would get a larger than normal bruise. At the time I didn't think much about it. I have always been clumsy, and when combined with a rocking boat, I was bound to get more bruises. By the end of our four-week adventure I was bruised and tired, but that wasn't unusual after a long dive trip.

————

I was back in Dr. Holland's office for a follow-up exam five days after returning from Indonesia. There was no change in my vision. In one respect that was good news; the dive vacation hadn't made things worse. However, it also meant that my vision wasn't getting better. The doctors had told me that my vision would probably never improve but I had hoped that they were wrong.

————

After a long dive vacation and as part of my personal health responsibility program, on Monday, July 30th, I went to my dermatologist, Dr. Said, for my biannual skin exam. My active life style forces me to spend a lot of time outside. I'm fair-skinned and until recently, I wasn't good about using sunscreen, which makes me a prime candidate for skin cancer. My family had been under Dr. Said's care for many years and she knew us well. During the exam, I told her about my eye occlusion. As I was checking out, she asked me to wait. Several minutes later she returned and handed me a piece of paper and said, "I think this is the name of your mystery disease." Dr. Said had given me a print-out of an online medical article about a man who had an eye occlusion and was subsequently diagnosed with Wegener's Granulomatosis.

As I read the article it was as if I was reading my own medical history. The similarities were uncanny. Over the years I had been told that I might have many things, but I'd never heard of Wegener's Granulomatosis. The name gave no clue as to what it might be. I needed to do some research, and I was good at online medical investigation. After several hours of searching, I had gathered information about the disease and I analyzed the current forms of treatment. The disease was a bad one, even deadly, and the medications to treat it had serious side effects. I told no one. Not even Larry. What if I didn't have this disease? There was no need to prematurely upset my family. I was seeing Dr. Gorn in a couple of days for my test results, I hoped he would know.

I sat down in Dr. Gorn's office on Wednesday, August 1st. He placed my medical file on his small desk. I had my own file folder containing my research sitting on my lap. I didn't wait. Why make him say the words? I wanted to save him, this one time, from having to tell a person such bad news. I handed him the paper that Dr. Said had given me. Dr. Gorn scanned it, set it aside, opened my medical file, and began going over the test results. I moved closer to him; I needed to see. And that afternoon, Dr. Gorn diagnosed me with Limited Wegener's Granulomatosis.

———

It's almost impossible to describe Wegener's Granulomatosis (WG). It is a rare, serious, complex disease that wears many masks. There is currently no known cause or cure, and if not treated, it can be life-threatening. Doctors and researchers believe that whatever causes WG seems to trigger the immune system to behave abnormally. It becomes overactive and begins a cascade of inflammatory reactions throughout the entire body. This inflammation can cause a wide range of problems such as: organ damage (most commonly the lungs and kidneys), inflammation of the blood vessels (vasculitis), and the formation of cell-clusters (granulomas) or nodules. This is an extremely simplified description of this obscure and serious disease. Bottom line – my immune system was attacking me!

Since there is no known cause for WG, doctors must be able to recognize the symptoms. But the symptoms are many and often more commonly associated with other medical issues. Among them: problems in the eyes, ears, and nose; persistent coughing; respiratory difficulties; voice or swallowing changes; blood in urine; kidney problems; joint pain; fatigue; and skin rashes or sores. But how do you piece these seemingly unrelated symptoms together? For example, I went to a nose specialist for my sinus problem and subsequent surgery; I saw an ophthalmologist for my vision problems; I visited a urologist for the blood in my urine; and a gastroenterologist for the atypical acid reflux that caused my cough and sore throat. These were all specialists who managed the problem that related to their area of expertise. But as it turned out, each of these "problems" was actually a signpost for a larger, more serious condition: Wegener's Granulomatosis. It's no wonder that I went undiagnosed for more than a decade. Now, I saw my situation from a different perspective. The vascular eye occlusion had actually been a gift. It was the clue that led to the diagnosis. I had traded some vision for life.

After Dr. Gorn confirmed that I had Wegener's, I felt relieved. The puzzle had been solved and I could begin treatment. Sure I was scared, but I would deal with that later. Right now I needed to decide on a treatment program. I use the word "treatment" because there is no cure. The goal was to use drugs to get me into remission. Dr. Gorn and I discussed the different medications: low-dose chemotherapy drugs (Cytoxan, methotrexate, Imuran) combined with corticosteroids (prednisone), and various immunosuppressants. I had already researched the drug options and was well aware of both their benefits and side effects.

I was diagnosed with *Limited* WG because I had no kidney or lung involvement. With that in mind, I told Dr. Gorn that I would not take certain medications because of the serious side effects. I looked into his eyes and calmly said, "If there's no life in life then I'm not interested." I could tell he was surprised by my comment, but he knew that I meant it. I had done my homework and had considered the risks verses the rewards of each drug. Dr. Gorn advised me of all the options and *together* we agreed on the drug I would try. Yes, I was taking a risk by not using a more aggressive drug treatment, but Dr. Gorn respected *my* choice. It was, after all, my life. To me, life meant more than just having a pulse, and I made an informed decision based on my personal situation.

———

I have no memory of telling Larry that I had been diagnosed with Wegener's Granulomatosis. So, as I was writing this book, I asked him if he remembered me telling him. Larry said that he did remember some things, only fragments. At first I was curious about what he remembered, but as I sat on our bedroom floor waiting for him to tell me, I felt a growing sense of unease.

Larry began describing what he remembered. He told me that I was emotional. I asked in what way. He said I was crying. He said that I had mentioned something about mortality – then I stopped him. Why was I doing this to us? For the details in a book! It was obvious that we had consciously or unconsciously placed this event in a deeply protected area of our minds, and I wasn't going to do anything more to bring it out. We'd already lived it once, and that was enough, for both of us.

———

On Friday, August 3rd, I drove up to Cal State Fullerton (where I teach) and met with Dr. Bill Beam. We had known each other for 16 years. We'd started as student (me) and teacher (him), but were now colleagues and friends. Dr. Beam was preparing to leave the university for a one-year sabbatical and I was taking over some of his responsibilities. We were meeting to discuss some final details.

Dr. Beam was my mentor and he knew me well. I needed to tell someone about the diagnosis, and I felt safe telling him. As we stood in the semidarkness of the Fitness Assessment Lab, I described in a very matter-of-fact way, my condition. The concern in his face was obvious. He asked, "Doesn't anything affect you?" I said, "Yes, but I keep going." I had to. What choice was there?

———

I was nine days into the drug regimen, and working at my computer when I began having difficulty focusing, but I didn't think much about it. I was getting dizzy from looking at the computer monitor, so I decided to take a short break. I went upstairs to grab a small gift bag, and on the way back down, my hand dropped the bag. Reaching with the same hand, I tried to pick it back up, but my hand dropped it again. Fascinating. My hand wasn't working. Then I felt my left cheek go numb. Now I knew what was happening. I had been certified to give electrocardiograms and had briefly worked for a cardiologist. I was having strokes! I started to monitor their timing and patterns, and asked Larry to drive me to the emergency room.

Larry dropped me off at the ER door, and went to park the car. I walked up to the check-in window and said, "I'm having strokes." The woman behind the desk handed me some paperwork to complete. I told her that I couldn't see and she said, "Well, do your best." I laughed, scribbled my name on the form, and gave it back to her along with my insurance card. Within minutes, Larry walked in and I was taken back. The hospital technician took my blood pressure and it was 181/101. Wow! I wondered what it was at home while I was having the strokes. After seven hours in the emergency room, I was admitted to Mission Hospital for acute transient ischemic attacks (TIA: mini-stokes).

Before allowing them to move me to the stroke unit, I politely but adamantly insisted on a private room. I was on a strong immunosuppressant drug and the hospital was full of sick people. I was prepared to walk out if they didn't give me my own room. I'll admit that I was scared but it wasn't because of the TIAs, it was because of my current environment, one of the world's deadliest, a hospital, and the harm it could potentially do me.

It was late by the time I was taken to a room. Larry was physically and emotionally exhausted. I had tried to send him home several times, but he refused to leave. During the hours of waiting, I distracted myself by observing and tinkering with the medical equipment. I knew how to use most of it and it kept me entertained. Larry, on the other hand, had nothing to do but worry. He felt helpless. As the nurse hooked me up to the IV and the other monitoring devices, I asked Larry if he could get me something to eat. I hadn't eaten since late morning and was hungry. He went to Carl's Jr. and brought me a chicken sandwich. I thanked him and he finally agreed to go home. I gave him a kiss good night and said I would call if there were any changes.

After Larry left I tried to eat the chicken sandwich, but I couldn't hold it. The inside of my arm felt like it was on fire! It was the IV. My blood vessels were so fragile that the vein the IV was in had burst and saline solution was filling my arm. It took two nurses and a phlebotomist 45 minutes to get the IV back into me. Each vein they tried just broke. Using a baby-size needle they finally got one in and working. My arms had so many bruises after all of the unsuccessful attempts that it looked like someone had beaten them with a baseball bat.

I didn't sleep. I kept thinking about the invisible damage inside my body. If the blood vessels were so fragile, what else might happen? Like the vascular occlusion in my eye, the TIAs were another sign of the covert workings of the disease. The nurse had told me that in the morning I would undergo several more tests: a CT Scan, brain MRI, cardio angiogram, carotid ultrasound, and blood and urine tests. They might supply more answers, and with a disease like Wegener's, answers were in short supply.

The long, sleepless night gave me time to think. The TIAs had not returned, and my blood pressure and oxygen saturation levels were normal. I now thought of the upcoming tests as an opportunity to have a hospital-grade physical exam. After all, I was still planning on climbing Mt. Aconcagua in December, and this was a great opportunity to find out where I stood on the medical platform of WG. I didn't have a death wish, and I wanted to make responsible decisions, but in order to do that, I needed answers. What caused the TIAs? Were there any abnormalities in my brain, heart, or other major blood vessels? It was great news – all the tests results came back normal. Relieved, I left the hospital.

———

The fall semester at CSUF started nine days after I was released from the hospital, and I had more than a full teaching load. The one time I decided to take on extra work, I was sick all day, every day. In an effort to control the disease, I had to take a strong medication to suppress my immune system. One side effect of the medication was severe nausea. As the semester passed, I had regular visits with Dr. Gorn and Dr. Holland. They monitored my progress and watched for damage caused by the disease and/or the drug. This type of medication couldn't be started at treatment strength; it would be too strong. So, I began on a low dosage and by the time I started to feel a little better, the dosage would be increased, which in turn would intensify the nausea. That's how it had to be done; month by month until I finally reached the treatment dosage of the drug.

I was continuously sick but the level of sickness varied. On good days, I'd only have nausea and severe fatigue. But because the medication lowered my body's natural defenses, it left the door wide open for infection. I was teaching five classes and coordinating a fitness testing lab. This meant that I interacted with about 150 students per teaching day. As a result, I was continuously sick from the illnesses that the students brought into the classroom. I remember one day I was so sick that I couldn't even sit in a chair. I had to hang onto my desk to keep from falling on the floor. But as sick as I was, and for as long as I was sick, I never missed a day of work. I had responsibilities, and I refused to be at home sick in bed. It was a battle of mind over matter.

———

Wegener's, the doctors, and the medications were now part of my life, but I wouldn't let them rule it. I wasn't about to allow the disease to become the writer and director of *The Life and Times of Cindy Abbott*. I had a mountain to climb, and Everest was what I focused on.

How was I going to manage the disease and train to climb Mt. Everest? I had just reached the treatment level of the drug that, hopefully, would control the disease. But I still felt the nausea daily, and now I had a suppressed immune system on top of that. I had only climbed Mt. Kilimanjaro, which didn't require any technical skills. I had so much to learn about mountaineering and I had to develop the physical strength needed to climb big mountains. Time, however, had run out. We were leaving for Argentina and Mt. Aconcagua in a week.

Then it hit me. I realized that how I approached Wegener's, was also the perfect approach to train for Mt. Everest. I would look at the big picture, break it into parts, and take it one step at a time. I called it my *10-feet-at-a-time* approach. I would observe how my body reacted and monitor my disease with each day and with each mountain.

Chapter 3

DON'T BREAK A LEG

Before I was diagnosed with Wegener's my original Everest climb-date was spring of 2011 or 2012. I needed time to both train and save money, but now things were different. Not knowing when or how the disease would manifest next, I set a new date - spring 2010. That gave me two and a half years to get my disease into remission, learn mountaineering skills, and come up with enough time and money to train. Was this crazy? Maybe. Was it possible? Well, there was only one way to find out. So, I took the first step and never looked back.

———

On December 28, 2007, Larry and I landed in Mendoza, Argentina. I had just recovered from a six-week battle with a respiratory infection, but was still experiencing the drug-induced nausea, and was physically weak from being so sick for so long. As I waited for my bags in the airport I thought about the events of the past six months and, so far, my *10-feet-at-a-time* approach was working. It had become a powerful tool for overcoming obstacles. "Don't look at the summit so high in the sky; just focus on the trail in front of your feet." I might be visually impaired and physically weak but I was about to climb the tallest mountain in South America, and I would do it *10-feet-at-a-time*.

Mendoza is a beautiful city filled with friendly people, and great food and wine. After checking into our hotel, we spent the afternoon running from agency to agency filing forms and getting our climbing permits. As it turned out, the cost of the permit included helicopter evacuation coverage. This meant nothing to me at the time, but it would later.

As the highest mountain outside of Asia, Mt. Aconcagua stands at an impressive 22,834 feet. Instead of the more crowded "Normal Route" (up and down the through the Horcones Valley), we would traverse the mountain starting up through the Vacas Valley to the beautiful but rugged Relinchos Valley and down through the Horcones Valley. The round-trip climb was scheduled to take about 16 days (which included extra days in case of weather issues). This would give me a chance to evaluate my body, the disease's reaction to extreme altitude, and the challenges of an extended climb.

The next morning we left Mendoza and drove to the rustic Penitentes resort located at about 9,000 feet. It's a popular starting point for climbing Aconcagua, and the first step in the acclimatization process. When ascending a mountain, it's very important to allow the body to adjust to the higher altitude. You accomplish this by gradual gains in altitude, and then stopping for a period of time to let the body adjust to each higher elevation. If you don't do this, you can develop a number of altitude-related problems; some minor and some potentially life-threatening. Acute Mountain Sickness (AMS) is the most common problem, and according to the Institute of Altitude Medicine, can cause headaches, loss of appetite, nausea and vomiting, weakness and fatigue, and trouble sleeping. Rare, more serious conditions can also develop: High Altitude Cerebral Edema (HACE) which is swelling of the brain, and High Altitude Pulmonary Edema (HAPE) in which the lungs fill with fluid. Both can be deadly without immediate medial attention. So, we stayed at the resort for two nights. One night probably would have been enough, but I wanted to be on the safe side. I had enough issues to manage, and didn't want more.

On December 31st, we left the Penitentes resort and started hiking up the desert-like Vacas Valley, shadowing the rushing waters of the Rio Vacas. The dry areas of the riverbed were covered with rocks of various size and color. While the hiking wasn't physically demanding, I quickly realized that my distorted vision was a definite problem. My eyes weren't detecting the detailed changes in the depth and color of the rocks. I would step and slip or step and trip. At home, I hadn't noticed this because the brain compensates for the missing information, which gave me the illusion that what I saw in my familiar surroundings was exactly correct, even though it wasn't.

The retinal vascular occlusion had created a hole in the focus point of my left eye, but fortunately I still had some peripheral vision. For the previous four months I had taught myself how to function with my reduced vision, but I had practiced on uniformly-colored, flat surfaces and evenly spaced steps (my home and work environment). Now I was hiking on multicolored, oddly shaped rocks and I had to see what was really there. Shortening my *10-feet-at-a-time* approach, I took each step slowly enough to glance up, then down, before placing my foot. I had to do this for each step I took, one misstep could result in a trip-ending injury. This considerably slowed my pace, but allowed me to move more safely up the valley.

Our gradual approach allowed me time to retrain my eyes and regain some strength, but I still suffered from nausea. Before we left for the trip, I had a long conversation with our guide, Scott, about my medical situation. He was concerned about my nausea because it's also one of the symptoms of altitude sickness. Scott asked how he would know the difference; it was a reasonable question. I explained that the nausea associated with altitude sickness suppresses appetite, but the nausea I feel from the drug doesn't. In fact, I feel better if I eat. I told Scott that I would know the difference, and would be able to tell him. Once on the mountain, we fell into a pattern of disclosure. Several times a day Scott asked how I was feeling and I would reply, "Fine" or "What's for dinner?" Our first night on the trail was New Year's Eve, and we celebrated with a meal of stuffing, canned turkey, and a cup of hot chocolate.

Scott Woolums is an extremely experienced high-altitude guide. He has led over 30 trips up Aconcagua, and knows *her* well. The mountain is referred to as "her" because most Indo-European languages (Spanish, Old English, Hindi, Portuguese, Russian, German, French, and Italian) assign either male or female gender to their nouns. In the case of Mt. Aconcagua, the Spanish word for mountain is "la montana," which is a female noun in that language. Other mountains are named after a person thus establishing their gender, and still many others remain gender-neutral despite their names.

As new climbers, Larry and I learned a great deal from Scott. We had summited Mt. Kilimanjaro a year earlier, but this was the first climb where we had to carry heavy packs and perform camp duties. The first order of business was setting up the tents and because of the unpredictable weather, this had to be perfect. A few loose lines and we could lose the tent. Next on the agenda was to fetch water. On a mountain with limited routes, climbers were forced together and sometimes we had to hike long distances to find a water source that wasn't contaminated. Still, we always treated our water. No way was I going to suffer the nausea, fever, and diarrhea that could result from drinking bad water. Scott handled the cooking, and he was good at it. For dinner one night he made pizza, what a treat!

———

I was fairing better than I expected. I experienced occasional headaches, usually in the mornings because the brain gets less oxygen while sleeping, but after getting up and moving around, the headaches went away. And the drug-induced nausea was tolerable. The trickiest task turned out to be managing my medications. Some drugs had to be taken several times over the course of the day while others could not be taken within a certain time of another drug. But the most important medication, the one that suppressed the Wegener's, was the most difficult to time. I had to take it twice a day, and I couldn't eat two hours before or one hour after I took it. This meant that I had to plan when I ate while climbing a big mountain. Not an easy task.

At lower altitudes, timing my medications around eating wasn't such an issue, but high on the mountain with my appetite suppressed by the effects of the altitude, and the more basic, less appetizing food (i.e., energy bars), eating became one of my biggest concerns. We hiked for five to six hours a day which used a lot of calories, and because I couldn't eat enough to replace those calories, I started losing weight as my body began to eat itself. I had to force myself to take every bite of food I could manage to get into my mouth and swallow. It was that difficult. And the higher we went, the harder it got. If I didn't eat, I wouldn't be able to summit.

———

The route we took up Aconcagua wasn't technically difficult but it was strenuous. Most of the hiking was on lose rocks called scree. The scree sat on top of hard-pan dirt resulting in unstable footing. Going up these steep scree slopes was slow and demanding. I would take one step up only to have my foot slide half way back down, it was very frustrating. I had to take two steps to get the distance of one. Going down the scree slopes was fast but dangerous. If the scree was deep enough, we used a plunge-type step and scree-skied down three to four feet with a single step. If the scree was shallow, the lose rocks on the hard dirt was similar to walking on slope covered with marbles. We had to be careful not to slip, it could be a long fall.

In addition to the risks associated with the extreme altitude, another major concern for climbers on this mountain is the weather. Aconcagua is famous for her erratic weather. Even in summer (December through February), storms and high winds can be devastating, even deadly, and climbers must remain vigilant to stay out of harm's way.

———

By the time we reached Camp 1 (16,300 ft) on January 5th, Scott was aware that high winds were predicted to hit the mountain in the next few days and last for many thereafter. Weather was always a concern on mountains and Scott's 35 years of experience was a valuable asset. That night at dinner, Scott talked to us about the situation and suggested that we modify our schedule and leave for Camp 2 (18,000 ft) a day early. We were going to try and get to High Camp before the winds.

On January 9th, we made our way into High Camp also known as White Rocks (19,200 ft). The winds started about the same time we arrived, so we quickly set up the tents then spent the next several hours building protective boulder walls round them. By the time we were done, the winds on the summit had reached 80 to 100 MPH. As planned, Scott got us up and into camp in time to weather the storm. Now we just had to wait for a break in the winds, which was supposed to come the next day or day after. We were in a perfect position to go for the summit, so we just stayed in our tent and waited.

Sleeping was all but impossible as the winds roared over our tent. As I lay in my sleeping bag I could hear the next gust coming up the mountain. As it got closer, it got louder and when it hit, the tent shook violently. The sound and power of the wind made me feel like I was under a speeding freight train. I kept my eyes fixed on the tent poles, waiting for them to snap. If the poles broke the tent would be ripped apart and everything in it blown away. The hours passed and our tent held fast.

At 2 AM Scott came over and told us we wouldn't be going for the summit, the wind was still too strong. By midmorning the wind had died down, and Scott said we would try again the next day. By now, Larry and I had already decided to abort the summit attempt. This was our first experience in these conditions and at such a high altitude, and we were not comfortable. Scott had set up a perfect summit plan and more experienced climbers may have had no issues, but we asked Scott to go down. I saw the surprise in his eyes but he understood our discomfort, so we packed up the camp and started down.

I was crossing a fairly steep scree slope at about 19,000 feet when I snagged one of my boots on the other and fell. How far? I don't know. As I tumbled down the side of the mountain I thought, "I have to stop myself." So I threw out my arms and legs, I rolled again, my foot dug into the ground and I heard the snap of my leg as I came to a stop. Okay, I knew my leg was broken but where? Using my trekking poles I pushed myself upright but fell back to the ground. Wow, that hurt! But now I knew where the break was, it was the lower part of my leg, the part inside my boot. I stood up again and did not sit down until I arrived at Plaza de Mules base camp 5 hours and 5,000 feet later.

———

People have since asked me, "How did you do that?" I was too high for helicopter evacuation so my choices were to sit there and freeze or get down that mountain, even if I had to crawl. Again I used the *10-feet-at-a-time* approach (just get ten feet closer and then think about what's next). That day, high on the mountain, I had somehow been able to put away the pain. I don't know where I put it, but for however long it took, the pain was irrelevant; it didn't get an opinion. I had to get off the mountain. But as I got closer to base camp and I realized that I was going to make it, the pain came out of hiding.

———

There was a doctor stationed at Plaza de Mules base camp (14,000 ft). He lived and worked in a one-room wooden shack. He slept on a bunk in the back near a small gas stove and operated from a single table with two chairs. There wasn't even a light bulb. After standing in line for two hours it was finally my turn. Now almost dark, the doctor had to leave the door open for light. In Spanish, he told me to remove my boot. I shook my head. He told me again, but I refused. There was no way I was removing that boot! I held up my foot and the doctor pulled it off – I cried out. The doorway had filled with the curious faces of waiting climbers but the doctor told them to move away, they were blocking his light. My leg looked as if it had been beaten with a baseball bat. It was swollen and a mixture of blue, black, yellow, and purple in color. The doctor confirmed that my leg was broken but informed me that the helicopter couldn't get me down because of the high winds. He said to come back in the morning but he doubted that it would be able to fly the next day either. I would just have to wait, maybe for days. On the bright side, the climbing permit covered the cost of the helicopter evacuation. I just wished he had some pain medicine, but he didn't. So, with the help of some passing climbers, I limped to our tent.

———

Later that evening I realized I had gotten down that mountain by tapping into an inner strength. The strength had always been there, waiting. I was weak from 11 days on the mountain and I had broken my leg, but I was smiling. I felt a new level of self-confidence. With the knowledge that I could tap into this inner reservoir of power, I believed the sky was my limit and climbing Mt. Everest was my chance to reach beyond the clouds.

———

By the time I got back to the United States my lower leg and foot were so bruised and swollen that I thought the skin was going to split! I went to an orthopedic surgeon who told me that I had a spiral fracture of the distal fibula and needed surgery to insert a metal plate and five screws to hold the bone together. Okay, but what about the Wegener's? I had climbed to almost 20,000 feet and had no problems with the disease, but surgery was another issue. Five months ago, when I was in the hospital, it had been almost impossible to get an IV in me. What would happen if I had surgery? So I said, "But I have Wegener's Granulomatosis." The surgeon replied, "Okay," and left the room. I got the distinct feeling that he had no knowledge of my disease; most doctors I met didn't. That evening the anesthesiologist called me; he knew about the disease. I felt better and said, "See you in the morning."

———

On January 24, 2008, two weeks after breaking my leg, I hobbled into Dr. Holland's office at Jules Stein Eye Institute. He looked at me and shook his head. While climbing Aconcagua I hadn't had any problems with my disease. Instead, I broke my leg. After all these years, he knew me. He knew I was a stubborn adventure-seeker who would not let this disease keep me from living my life. I was always responsible about my medical care and what else could he say, so he didn't.

Dr. Gorn, my rheumatologist, didn't know me as well and was quite concerned about my situation. I had only been at treatment level of the medication for a few months, wasn't in remission, and was now having surgery. He didn't say as much but I know he thought I was crazy; I could see it in his eyes. As the years passed and I continued my adventures, he accepted who I was and my approach to life.

————

I learned a lot about high-altitude mountain climbing from our experience on the windy, scree slopes of Mt. Aconcagua, and I also realized that I had only touched the tip of the mountaineering world. If I was going to climb Mt. Everest, I had two years and three months and a lot to learn. But I was temporarily grounded by a cast and a broken leg. So I got out the books. I studied weather, snow, and avalanche patterns; practiced knot-tying; and the principles of mountaineering skills such as mixed ice/rock climbing, ropes and anchors, and navigation. I would put these into practice when the cast came off.

————

We plan our vacations well in advance, usually years ahead. Our next trip was scheduled for late June to go hiking and climbing in Switzerland. But the condition of my leg was going to significantly limit my ability to climb. So we changed our vacation from climbing in the Alps to diving in Iceland. On our way to Iceland we planned a stop in Boston to visit some of Larry's family and high school friends. I had never been to this part of the country; it sounded like fun.

We arrived in Boston on June 10th. I had completed 10 weeks of physical therapy but my ankle was still locked-up, and by the end of each day the pain had my full attention. I knew it would get better with time but I was on a training schedule. My doctor said that I was healing well and cleared me for diving and hiking. So after visiting some friends and family, we drove to New Hampshire and climbed 4,000 feet up Tuckerman's Ravine to the summit of Mt. Washington. My leg barked at me the entire time, but too bad, it didn't get a vote. I had to regain my mobility and climbing was my version of accelerated physical therapy.

———

From Boston we flew to Iceland. What a beautiful country, especially in the summer. With 23 hours of daylight, we were on the move. My foot complained but I ignored it. Larry had always wanted to dive in the Silfra Crack, a World Heritage Site, where divers can reach out and touch both the American and Eurasian continental plates at the same time. We made three dives in this 37 degree water; I was 5 degrees from becoming an ice cube. It was the first time the doctor allowed me to walk wearing the 60 pounds of diving equipment; I was making progress. After a wonderful week in Iceland, we flew back to Boston, had lunch at Cheers, went to Fenway Park for a Red Sox' game, and returned home the next day.

I'm not cold, I'm not cold, I'm not cold!

We'd been home for nine days and were in a local pet store buying cat food when I walked past the cat adoption cages. I never look; it's too dangerous. But this time I glanced, and in the corner of the window I saw a tiny, funny face rolling around and around. I went over to Larry and said, "You have to see this. But just walk past and don't stop." But he stopped. Three days later we were the proud parents of the cutest and strangest 8-week old kitten. The adoption papers said her name was Rosebud. Are you kidding me? She was no Rosebud! She had tortoiseshell markings and this unusual line down the middle of her nose. It looked familiar. I went into the office and examined the picture we had just hung of the Silfra Crack, that was it. The line on her nose was the exact shape of the famous Icelandic landmark and her name became Silfra.

The newest member of our family.

The plate in my leg bothered me from the moment it was put in. The skin in that area is very thin and when I hiked, my boot rubbed against the plate, and I could feel a tendon catching on the end of it. That couldn't be good. On August 4th, I had a second surgery; this time to remove the metal plate and screws. I was back in a cast but at least the metal was out of my leg (it's now mounted on my office wall above the picture of Larry and I that was taken on Aconcagua a few hours before I fell, and makes for a great conversation piece).

Seven weeks later, on September 28, 2008, I summited Mt. Whitney (14,504 ft). My leg was mad at me, but it still got no say, time was not on my side. I'd already lost part of my vision. When would I lose more or all of it? What other things were going to happen? I didn't know and the doctors couldn't say. And the broken leg had cost me precious time. So, I trained every day I could and with every dollar we could spare.

———

Life is intriguing. Do things happen for a reason or do they just happen? Why did I get diagnosed with a rare disease just months after deciding to climb Mt. Everest? Why did I fall and break my leg? I cannot say nor do I care, they happened and I move on. What I care about is "why" wasn't my disease detected sooner, and "why" when I tell most doctors that I have Wegener's, do they not know anything about it? It's scary! I'm not blaming anyone. I am simply telling my story, but as it turns out, it's not just *my* story.

———

I found two fantastic resources as I continued researching WG: the National Organization of Rare Disorders (NORD), the leading advocate for all people with rare diseases/disorders, and the Vasculitis Foundation (VF), which represents the 15 vasculitis-related rare diseases including Wegener's Granulomatosis. Both of these nonprofit, patient-advocacy agencies offered a wealth of information. Hour after hour, day after day, I scoured through their material. I had no idea there were so many people affected by rare diseases.

According to the National Organization of Rare Disorders (NORD), a rare disorder is one that affects less than 200,000 Americans and there are about 6,000 rare disorders that affect about 30 million Americans. NORD also states that of the 6,000 rare disorders, only about 200 of them have FDA-approved treatments. That leaves 5,800 disorders and 20 million people without approved therapies. If so many people suffer from these diseases, why aren't there more treatments? NORD, along with many other individuals and organizations, are working tirelessly to rectify the situation.

NORD has been fighting for Americans with rare disorders since 1983 with the enactment of the *Orphan Drug Act.* On June 29, 2010, NORD's Chair of the Board went before the FDA to present a proposal of changes needed to help stimulate therapy development. The changes are far-reaching and multi-faceted. Some of the key participants include the FDA, academic researchers, pharmaceutical companies, and financial companies. The issues surrounding rare disease research and drug development are complex and beyond the scope of this book. But what I can say is that there are many people with rare disorders who do not have time – they need help now, and NORD is working hard to get them that help.

The Vasculitis Foundation (VF) is a patient support organization founded it 1986 by a woman with Wegener's Granulomatosis. The VF provides patients, family members, and the medical community with much needed resources. When I was diagnosed with WG I felt alone with this very serious disease, my family was scared, and it was a difficult time. Then I found the VF and I became part of a family of people with similar wants, needs, and fears. I wasn't alone after all.

The collective work of both NORD and the VF have made a world of difference for patients and their families by providing resources, education, support services, advocacy, and research funding. Another key area they strongly target is raising awareness about rare disorders. Most people, including doctors, are unaware of the existence of these diseases. If doctors have no knowledge of the diseases, how can they hope to diagnose them? Think of the number of known diseases and disorders, it baffles the mind. Now add 6,000 rare disorders. How can doctors keep up? But it gets worse. Just look at one rare disease – mine. Wegener's Granulomatosis manifests in so many different ways it's no wonder people like me go undiagnosed for years, and for some it's too little, too late.

––––

If I look back at the years I spent trying to get answers and watching my health decline, I could get angry, very angry. As it turned out, there was an answer but no one had recognized the mysterious clues. So the damage continued and with the loss of my sight the answer was found. I wasn't angry then nor am I now, but I did feel the need to do something to help the next person get diagnosed sooner.

In the spring of 2009, I contacted NORD and the VF. They had already started a national and international awareness movement. Their mottos are: *Alone we are Rare, Together we are Strong* (NORD), and *Sticking Together for a Cure* (VF). After several calls and e-mails, my 2010 Mt. Everest climb changed from a personal challenge to a campaign to raise rare disease awareness and show people the importance of following their dreams. I was going to stand on the top of the world holding a NORD banner.

––––

Going public with my very personal story was scary. Up to this point, I had told very few people I had Wegener's and now I was about to tell the world. I discussed it with my husband and daughter as they would also be affected. I had already decided to climb Mt. Everest, I was in remission, and in an effort to raise rare disease awareness, I launched my website.

All of our stories are different yet similar, which is why I titled my website "Reaching Beyond the Clouds." It is a metaphor that applies to every person, every day. We all have needs, goals, and dreams both large and small, and reaching these may be a one of choice or one of necessity.

In December, with the help of Mimi Ko Cruz, from the Office of Public Affairs at California State University, Fullerton, the first press release went out and others soon followed. I would use the media attention and the Mt. Everest climb to help raise rare disease awareness and show people that there is hope. For some, climbing a flight of stairs is their Mt. Everest.

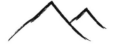

Chapter 4

THE POWER OF SUPPORT

A good man is hard to find but 25 years ago I found a great one. Not only do we have the same interests, morals, and values, we also both love to experience new things, people, and places. From our work to our play, we do everything together. We are soul mates – together always, even when we are apart.

One thing we both love is ballroom dancing. We started taking lessons in 1999 in preparation for our first cruise ship vacation – ten days on the Panama Channel for the Millennium New Year's Eve. After that cruise, dancing became a weekly part of our lives. For years we took lessons and practiced; we weren't great dancers, but we had fun. We could be anywhere, in an airport waiting for a flight or at some remote resort after a day of diving or hiking, and if a song came on that we liked, we'd get up and dance. One evening after dinner in the basement restaurant of a small lodge in the Russian village of Cheget, Larry and I were sitting at our table when a cha-cha song started to play. I asked Larry to dance, and with no other diners in the restaurant, we got up and danced. One by one the staff peeked out from behind the door, smiling as they watched. From that night on, after the other guests left, they played that song and we would dance.

Dancing at Larry's retirement party!

———

My daughter, Teshia, is loving, caring, and very giving of herself; a mother could not ask for a better child. Like us, she is also an adventure seeker and has a special love for animals. In 2008, Teshia took a semester off college and went to Zimbabwe for a month to volunteer at a lion reserve. Whether by nature or nurture, she follows in my footsteps: traveling, exploring, and living life.

When I first told Teshia about my decision to climb Mt. Everest she was furious with me. She had seen the same television show that had inspired me, but it had the opposite effect on her. She knew climbing Mt. Everest was dangerous and didn't want to lose her mother. Teshia was so upset about the idea that she refused to discuss it. When I tried she would say, "I don't want to hear it!"

After about a year, Teshia came to terms with the fact that I was going to climb Mt. Everest. She realized that I was doing everything possible to be safe and responsible. Now that we could talk about my upcoming climb, I asked for her help. In the past, when Larry and I were away on one of our adventures, Teshia would run the household. This time I would be gone for 60 days and I needed her help more than ever. While Larry could handle the finances and our tax business; household duties, which he'd never done, might be a problem. I knew I was asking a lot of Teshia. She had her own life, school, and job to manage, but she agreed to help. Not only did Teshia help with the household duties, she also helped with my rare disease awareness campaign.

After I left for Mt. Everest I had little, and sometimes no, ability to update my website or Facebook page. So during my climb, Teshia along with my webmaster, Derrick Brown, and a close family friend, Stacie Parra, became my Internet advocates, allowing people to follow my journey.

———

Normally, Larry and I plan our travel around our finances. We work hard and live comfortably, but are by no means wealthy. For most of our 25 years together, we've both worked several jobs while running our own income tax business. Our jobs pay for the cost of daily life, and the income tax business provides for both unexpected expenses and our travel. In this way, we balance our living expenses and our travel costs.

When I made my decision to climb Everest, I had four to five years to save money. I figured it wouldn't be a problem; it would just take some extra planning. We could still adventure travel, we'd just have to opt for the less expensive trips on our list, and work in some mountain climbing along the way. With that plan, I determined that with a projected climb date, I'd have the money, equipment, and training I needed.

But everything changed after I was diagnosed with Wegener's Granulomatosis. I didn't know how much time I'd have before the disease made it impossible for me to climb Everest, so I moved up my climb date to 2010. Larry was afraid of what might happen, but he stood behind me and my dream. He selflessly put everything he wanted to do on hold. He placed our future travel list inside the world atlas, closed it, and put the atlas away. For the next three years, our travel was guided by my training schedule.

———

In the summer of 2008, I was feeling better and ready to begin the application process to join an Everest climbing team. Scott, the guide with whom I was training, didn't know if he would be going back to Everest in 2010, so I contacted Russell Brice, the owner of Himex. It was his company and climbers that were the focus of Discovery Channel's *Everest: Beyond the Limit* (my original inspiration to climb Everest), and I felt that I had some insight into Russell's operation. After many calls, e-mails, and forms, I was accepted to his 2010 Mt. Everest

Team. I still have the e-mail stating: "Welcome to the team." What an awesome feeling. I was really going to do it! I was going to climb to the top of the world!

———

Mt. Everest is almost exclusively summited via two routes: through Tibet (China) from the north, and Nepal from the south. Russell had been operating Everest expeditions from Tibet, the north side, for over 12 years, but in late 2008 he transferred his operation to Nepal, the south side. Many other Everest operators/climbers also switched from climbing Tibet's north side to Nepal's south side. This change was largely due to the uncertain access to Everest from the north side (mostly stemming from political issues that are beyond the scope of this book). I contacted Russell to confirm that we would be climbing from the south in 2010, he said yes, and with that answer, the cost of climbing Mt. Everest jumped by $20,000! Logistics were a major factor in the cost increase. The south-side climbing permit was $10,000 per person! Great, now I had to come up with even more money.

———

In the summer of 2009 I did my final big-mountain training climbs in preparation for Everest, and Larry went with me. We started by summiting Washington's Mt. Rainier (14,411 ft). Three weeks later we met Scott in Russia and summited Mt. Elbrus (18,513 ft). From there we flew to Kyrgyzstan and climbed to 22,500 feet on Peak Lenin (we had to abort the summit attempt due to weather). It was during that trip that Scott told me he would be guiding a trip to Everest in 2010. By then I had been training with Scott for over two years and he was familiar with my physical, mental, and climbing abilities. It seemed reasonable that if I was going to climb Everest, it should be with Scott, but I was already signed-up with Russell Brice and my deposit was nonrefundable. What a quandary. I felt that I had a better chance of summiting if I climbed with Scott since he knew me, but I'd have to forfeit the money already paid to Russell, which meant coming up with even more money to join Scott's team. Success verses money!?!

After returning home from the summer climbing trip, I contacted Russell and explained my situation. The contract I signed clearly stated that my deposit was not refundable and I understood why. Everest expeditions are planned well in advance and the operators incur many expenses that the deposits are used to help pay. Russell was under no obligation to return any portion of the money I had paid him, but he did. He returned every penny! I thanked him with all of my heart.

With Everest seven months away, I was now on *Mountain Trip's 2010 Summit Team*. Scott had partnered up with Todd Rutledge and Bill Allen (co-owners of Mountain Trip International) and together had formed a team of five Everest climbers. This was perfect; a small team with Scott as expedition leader. But time and money were in short supply, so I trained locally on Mt. Baldy (10,064 ft).

Standing on the summit of Mt. Baldy with my ice ax and medication. (Photo by Larry Abbott)

———

In the fall of 2009, I started experiencing pain in the joints of my left foot. For months I tried treatment after treatment, but nothing helped. The pain got so bad that I started to limp. If I couldn't walk, how was I going to climb? Dr. Gorn ordered an MRI, and the results showed unexplainable fluid accumulation, inflammation, and arthritis developing in the joints of my foot. The disease had struck again! Dr. Gorn told me that if I continued ballroom dancing I probably wouldn't be able to climb Mt. Everest. So after 10 years, we danced no more.

———

The combination of the earlier climb date and the increased cost of climbing the south side severely tipped our financial planning scale. I struggled with this new development. Could I really be so selfish? I just couldn't imagine putting us into this kind of financial situation. We had always been so careful with our finances. If I did this, it would take years to recover, but I also knew that if I didn't go to Everest in 2010, I never would.

Grasping for anything to help salvage my dream, I came up with a plan. I would cash-out one retirement account and take a loan from another, but that still wasn't enough. I had climbed mountains carrying heavy packs, but the weight of this financial burden was crushing me. While Larry didn't understand my drive to climb Everest, he did recognize how important it was to me, and he came to my rescue by offering to take a loan from his retirement account. This was a huge decision for Larry. He had spent the past 40 years meticulously planning for our financial future. But silently I think we both came to the same conclusion: I should spend my retirement now, while I could still enjoy it – the Wegener's could change everything in an instant.

My dream was safe, at least from the financial perspective, but the loans had to be repaid. So, as I continued preparing for Everest, I also searched for financial alternatives. My first thought was to look for a sponsor or sponsors. I had no idea how to go about this, but I thought that companies might be interested in both my unique situation and raising rare disease awareness. I applied to mountaineering equipment and clothing companies and other large corporations who offered grants, sponsorships, and stewardships in the interest of giving back to the community. How naive I was.

After spending six months filing form after form and waiting for replies that sometimes never came, I realized that I didn't fit their business model. One of the largest clothing and equipment companies told me that they only provide for "their own athletes"; in other words, the industry's elite who looked the best and performed the best. They were not interested in real people with real lives. Other companies simply stated, "We do not sponsor individuals." My two final attempts were made in an effort to get a couple of major pieces of gear sponsored, each costing in the neighborhood of $1,000. One of the companies I contacted never even responded to my application. The other company was honest and told me that they didn't need additional marketing in that area, but good luck. From my perspective, sponsoring me seemed like an excellent business decision. It was an opportunity to show people the heart and spirit of the company. Silly me. They weren't interested in helping unless it benefited their pocketbook. One company, however, did show its heart and spirit: Mountain Tools, an independent mountaineering company. They gave me a generous discount on some gear, and I was (and still am) very grateful.

———

Since 1996, I have had the privilege of teaching Kinesiology and Health Science courses at California State University, Fullerton. I first stepped onto the campus as a student in the spring of 1990. I will never forget my first instructor,

Dr. Weinmann, who later became the chairperson for my master's thesis, which was published in the *International Journal of Sport Psychology*. As a person and a student I thrived in the university environment. The passion for exploring new ideas and the love of learning became infused into my veins, and at the age of 31, I found myself. I eventually transitioned from student to part-time faculty. I love my job and I could not imagine doing anything else. To me, the students, staff, and faculty at CSUF are extended family.

———

Larry and I usually scheduled our travel during school breaks, but there was a timing conflict between the CSUF semester schedule and the Mt. Everest trip. The Everest climbing season was a specific, once-a-year event and happened to fall during the last half of the spring semester. How was I going to mange this? I couldn't risk losing my job to climb a mountain.

One day, during a break between classes, I was talking with another faculty member when Dr. Koser walked into the room. Dr. Koser had been a kinesiology/health science professor, became the department chairperson, and was now the Associate Dean of the College of Health & Human Development. She had just returned from a research sabbatical in Nepal and was curious about my interest in climbing Mt. Everest. During our conversation I asked Dr. Koser if she thought it would be possible for me to co-teach classes for one semester. She thought it was, and told me to discuss the issue with Dr. McMahan, the current chair of the Health Science Department.

I made an appointment with Dr. McMahan. This was a big step. So far everything I had done to prepare for climbing Mt. Everest in 2010 could be reversed, but the teaching schedules are made far in advance, and getting the approval to miss part of the school semester would make climbing Everest all the more real. It was scary to actually start the process of leaving the university and my job to climb Mt. Everest.

———

While there are too many people to individually thank for their support, I must acknowledge the students, staff, and faculty at California State University, Fullerton. They rallied behind me and my Everest goal. Through the efforts of Dr. McMahan and the administrative staff, I was scheduled to co-teach my spring semester classes. I would teach the first half and then turn my classes over to another instructor. It worked out perfectly.

———

The semester passed quickly and before I knew it, I was into my last two weeks of teaching. I had been so busy with work, training, and other preparations, time had literally evaporated. I was about to teach my last classes, and then I'd be on my way to Everest. It was an odd feeling. For the past 14 years I always had my teaching, and had never missed any part of a semester! I felt like a mother hen leaving her chicks before they were grown.

As I prepared for my departure, there was a covert operation in progress. On March 3rd while gathering my teaching materials after the day's lectures, the classroom began to fill with students, staff, and faculty. I had been set-up for a surprise going away party. I was overwhelmed by emotion as I was presented with the most beautiful bouquet of flowers I had ever seen along with a presentation board-sized card filled with wonderful words of encouragement and support. Then Dr. Beam, my friend and mentor, put his arm around my shoulder, and handed me a check for $2,000! It was made out to "Cindy Abbott's Adventure to Mount Everest," and signed, "Your Friends." I cried.

———

The following week Larry was walking from the kinesiology/health science office to teach his SCUBA class when he called me at home. "You'll never believe what is going on" he said. "There's a huge table full of all kinds of goodies being sold to raise money for your climb!" What! "Check your e-mail," he said. "Linda is sending you pictures." Sure enough, I had just received an e-mail about a bake sale in progress and it was beautifully done. The bake sale had been organized on short notice by one of my former students, Jordan Aquino, then-President of the Eta Sigma Gamma Honor Society, with the help of staff and other students. I was taken by surprise again, and felt humbled by their support.

March 17th was my last day of teaching, and I was both excited and sad. I taught my classes and said goodbye to my students. I packed up my briefcase and went outside to meet Jordan. He wanted to say goodbye and present me with a check from the proceeds of the bake sale. We sat on a bench outside the office and talked for a while. I gave him a hug, and crying, I walked off campus.

———

Everything was ready, but was I? The 66-day journey was a huge commitment. I had already put us into the financial position of taking out loans. I would be abandoning personal and professional responsibilities, risking my health, possibly my life, and putting my family through many hardships. Was reaching the summit of Mt. Everest worth so much?

Chapter 5

TO EVEREST

It seemed as if I was in a time warp. Yesterday Everest was a surreal dream on the distant horizon, a far away fantasy. Today, the mountain materialized in my every thought and action. I worked day and night tying up loose ends, doing everything possible to make my leaving easier for Larry and Teshia. But no matter what I did, I couldn't lighten the tremendous weight I felt on my heart. I was leaving and soon.

Despite the extreme physical demands of the Everest climb, I knew the emotional aspect was going to be the most difficult part of my journey. Could my spirit, my power, survive without my family near me? After months of soul-searching, I was still unsure how I'd endure the separation from the loves of my life.

To save money I had used frequent flyer miles to purchase my plane ticket, and because of the limited seat availability, I had to take a flight that would arrive in Kathmandu two days before the rest of the climbing team. When I initially booked the flight, 10 months previously, I didn't think twice about arriving two days early. Now, just five days before I was scheduled to leave, those two days were 48-hours of precious time that I could be at home with my family. I wanted, needed, that time.

In desperation, I started calling the airline to see if I could catch a later flight. I called early in the morning and late at night. Sometimes I got up in the middle of the night to call, but I always got the same answer – no. Still I kept calling. I had this feeling that somehow, if I kept trying, I would get that later flight. I needed another day at home, just one more day. I picked up the phone one last time, and without thinking my fingers dialed the number. Again I asked if there was an opening, and this time I got a different answer. One seat in First Class had become available and I had enough airline miles to get it! I couldn't believe it! I got to stay home an extra 24 hours!

———

Those last few days passed quickly and I was thankful for that extra time with my family, but it was now April 1st and after years of medical issues, training, planning, and preparing, it was time to leave. It was a difficult day on so many levels. I did two media interviews, went to see my doctor, worked out, finished packing, cleaned the house, hit the grocery store, said goodbye to my cats, and received a hug from my daughter that would have to last the next two months.

As Larry drove me to the airport there was an enigmatic, almost cryptic feeling between us. We chatted about meaningless things but for most of the drive, we were silent. How strange. I had imagined our last hours together filled with hugs, talking, holding hands, and powerful feelings, but it was just the opposite. I felt disconnected, as if I was already gone. Maybe we both had unconsciously begun the process of being separated, a form of self-protection. But we still had to endure our goodbye at the airport. I was filled with dread. We had never said goodbye to each other; we had always left together.

The airport was very quiet. It was late and my flight didn't leave for another three hours. We had planned to eat dinner together once I checked in, but there were only a handful of fast-food places still open, none very appetizing. We ordered some food, but just picked at it as we sat at a small table within view of the departure area. Neither of us knew what to say, and the longer we sat watching people leave, the more intense the sadness became. I looked into Larry's eyes, and I could see how tired and sad he really was. I was too, not to mention worried, and wondering whether Larry would be okay while I was gone. Sitting there at the airport, he looked different, like a hollow version of himself. I couldn't prolong this any further. I asked him to walk me to the security area; I could barely speak the words.

———

I arrived at the Yak and Yeti Hotel in Kathmandu late on the night of April 3ʳᵈ. Standing in my room, exhausted and excited, I felt changed. During the long flights and airport delays, I had shed the concerns of my normal life. There was no "normal" here, only intrigue. I walked over and opened my windows to breathe in the air; the air of a new world, a new adventure, and the new experiences awaiting me.

It was 2 AM in Kathmandu. I opened a bottle of wine that I had picked up in the Hong Kong duty-free, and poured a glass. As I sipped my wine, I sent Larry and Teshia each text messages letting them know that I had arrived and was relaxing in my room. For the next few days we would be able to communicate through text-messaging and e-mail (when the Internet connection worked). In a dreamlike haze of exhaustion, I stretched out on the large soft bed, and while waiting for their replies, I fell asleep.

———

I woke up to Easter Sunday and my first thoughts were of home. I checked my cell phone and had received messages from both Larry and Teshia. That felt good. I was half a world away but there they were – on my phone. I kissed my phone and kept it close.

At breakfast I ran into Scott. He had arrived several days earlier to manage the thousands of details surrounding the expedition. As he went about his business, I explored the hotel.

Still exhausted and jet-lagged, I spent most of the morning in the beautiful hotel garden surrounded by flowers, flowing fountains, and ancient temples. As Dorothy from *The Wizard of Oz* would say, "Toto, we're not in [California] anymore."

By late afternoon I had recovered enough to get my computer set up and online so I could send e-mails and update my website. That turned out to be quite a task between the sporadic Internet connection and the power outages. I wanted to contact Larry and Teshia as much as possible before we left for the trek to Base Camp as communication from that point on would be severely limited. Having just arrived and all alone, I needed to feel that we were still connected even though I was half a world away. Unfortunately, the time difference caused a delay in communication. I was 12 hours and 45 minutes ahead of California time. It was frustrating. I was lonely and desperate to hear from my family, but because of the time difference, I would have to wait until late at night or even the next morning to receive a reply. And soon I would no longer be able to receive their e-mails or text messages; we were leaving for Base Camp in three days. That evening I didn't feel like leaving my room so I ordered some soup and a salad and ate alone. I still hadn't left the confines of the hotel, maybe tomorrow.

———

The next day I woke up before 4 AM and checked my e-mail. Larry had sent a message that he had gone for a hike and found my note. Before I left, I had made a paper-heart love note and put it in his hiking boot. I didn't know when he would find it, but I knew he would eventually. Larry taped it to our bathroom mirror so he could see that my heart was always with him. Happy, I went down to breakfast and met Scott again. He told me that Jona-Marie, a trekking member, was also here and that we'd meet up with her later and all walk into town for lunch.

Kathmandu was a fascinating city; a noisy, colorful place filled with a mixture of cultures, customs, and religions both ancient and modern. The timeworn streets were jammed with a tangled frenzy of cars, bikes, motorcycles, and rickshaws. Crossing a street was a real challenge, like playing a game of chicken. There was a lot of horn blowing but whoever made the first move usually won. I got pretty good at it.

Jona-Marie and I hit it off right away. She was intelligent, funny, and full of energy, just what I needed. After lunch, Scott left us to conduct more business. So Jona-Marie and I walked around, dodging vehicles and taking pictures. The streets were lined with wooden poles holding massive tangles of all kinds of wires. No wonder the Internet and electricity was so erratic. I took a picture, and called it "crazy wires." It's one of my favorites from the trip.

Crazy wires in Kathmandu.

After we returned to the hotel, I borrowed one of Scott's satellite phones and spent the next two hours setting up my account and learning how to use it. This would be one of the only forms of communication from the mountain and I wanted to make sure that it worked. My first call was to Larry. I was so excited to hear his voice. Then I realized that it was the middle of the night at home. Oops! I wasn't used to calculating the time difference but he didn't care. We didn't talk for long; I wanted to save my satellite minutes for when I didn't have Internet access. My spirit was lifted after hearing Larry's voice. I ate dinner alone again, but this time I left my room and went down to the hotel restaurant. After eating, I spent the rest of the night sending e-mails. I had to make the best use of the time; in two days I would be away from civilization for almost two months.

———

I woke up at 3 AM and went to check my e-mail. The Internet was down and the business center didn't open for six hours. What if Larry or Teshia had sent me a message? Now I couldn't reply until they were asleep. I was so sad. At this point, hours mattered but there was nothing I could do. I kept myself distracted by packing my bags. I had to separate my mountain climbing gear, which would go straight to Base Camp, from my trekking gear, which I would take with me on the 10-day hike to Base Camp. This kept me busy but I still missed Larry. I couldn't stop thinking about what he might be doing at home "right now." I was trying to stay mentally connected with him for as long as possible. If that Internet would just work!

I ran into Scott in the hotel lobby, and he told me that everyone in the group had arrived: the 2010 Mountain Trip Everest Team was complete. There were five climbers (three females, two males), five trekkers (all female), and two guides (Scott and Bill). The women definitely ruled this trip! We all met for dinner at the hotel buffet. Everyone was friends with one or more individuals in the group with the exception of Jona-Marie and me. We were the odd-ones-out, but based on first impressions, this was going to be a fun group. Most of them had flown in that day and were tired, so after eating we disbanded to our rooms.

———

I woke up at 4 AM the morning before we left for Base Camp. I was finally adjusting to the time difference, not! As usual, the first thing I did was check my computer. Yay! I had received an e-mail from Larry. What a great way to start the day.

The Base Camp bags had left the night before, so we spent most of our last day in Kathmandu sightseeing. It was nice to get acquainted with the members of the group; they all seemed very likeable. After returning from our tour, everyone was busy making the final preparations for Everest. We were flying to Lukla in the morning. This was it. After years of planning I was literally about to take my first step toward the summit of Everest. I still couldn't believe that Larry wasn't with me but he was stuck at home, busy with our tax business and his teaching, while I was about to embark on an adventure of a lifetime.

It was now early evening in Kathmandu. I checked my e-mail, nothing from Larry. I was getting upset because I would have very limited contact after this. The group went into town for dinner. I went with them but left early so I could get back to the hotel and check for e-mails. None. I knew Larry was busy but I was leaving early in the morning, and I missed him so much already. Crying, I went to sleep.

———

I woke up at 4 AM and checked my computer one last time; still no email from Larry. Sad, I packed my computer and went to the hotel lobby to meet the group. We were flying to Lukla, and it was time to leave.

———

Every part of the Everest experience can be described as follows: get ready, hurry up, go, well maybe, no wait. And getting to Lukla was the first of many such events. We arrived at the airport at 6:30 AM for the one-hour flight, but bad weather had all the flights temporarily grounded. We waited almost six hours, and finally boarded the plane at 2 PM. We had a quick, by Nepal standards, lunch in Lukla and at 4 PM we left for the four-hour hike to the lodge at 11,400 feet. Those first steps on the trail were magical, and it was hard to believe that just nine days later I'd be at Mt. Everest Base Camp. I was finally on my way to the top of the world.

———

During the trek to Base Camp we hiked through the valleys of the Solo Khumbu region to the snow-capped mountains of the Himalayas. There were no roads, only trails, and the only way in or out was by foot (with the exception of an occasional helicopter). Food and supplies were transported by porters, small horses, cows, or large, hairy yaks. The local people had lived this agrarian way of life for centuries. The trails and villages were brought to life by the prayer flags and mani stones that reflected the culture and spirituality of the Nepalese. The mani stones varied from smaller flat stones to large boulders and were painted with sacred mantras. In acknowledgement of the local custom, we walked to the left of a mani stone. During those days, I had the opportunity to learn about and experience their blending of Buddhism and animist beliefs (that all things have a soul, including Mt. Everest).

———

A typical trekking day started with repacking our sleeping bags and personal items, followed by breakfast, and then a four to five hour hike to the next destination where we would spend the night in a small, rustic lodge. These lodges were full of local color and, for the most part, similar in offerings and design. There was usually a main room with picnic-bench tables and chairs, and a yak-dung burning stove (the only source of heat). The sleeping rooms were very basic: plywood walls, two wooden planks covered with a pad and a blanket (which if you were smart, you didn't use), and a single window for light. Once it got dark, headlamps were the only source of lighting. The toilet situation varied from a connected backroom to an outside shed, but they were almost always pit-toilets and if you didn't have your own toilet paper, then you were out of luck. As for the bathing accommodations, those ranged from a bucket of cold water with a tin can to an actual shower with hot water. The cost of having hot water, a luxury, varied according to the facility and the altitude. The higher the altitude, the longer it took to heat water. How much I paid to bathe depended on many factors, and hot water was one, but not necessarily the most important. Sometimes the length of time I went without bathing overruled all other factors. The lodges were part of the trekking experience and any lack of luxury was easily over looked by the scenery. Every day I opened my eyes to some of the most beautiful views in the world.

———

As we gained altitude, each stop was planned to allow our bodies to acclimatize. The higher we went, the fewer the oxygen molecules in each breath we took. For this reason, we stayed two nights in Namche at 11,300 feet where there each breath contained only 67% of the oxygen molecules as compared to sea level. During that time, our bodies were busy making more red blood cells to increase our blood's oxygen-carrying ability.

Namche Bazaar.

From Namche we hiked to Khumjung Village, which is just under 13,000 feet (63% oxygen), and it was there that we came face-to-face with the potentially deadly effects of altitude. As we sat around our table playing cards, two men came into the room with a woman who could barely walk. Her skin was ashen grey and although open, her eyes were empty. The men didn't speak any language I could understand, but it was obvious that the woman was very ill. They had come from higher up and this was as far as they could get. Of all the lodges in the area, luck had brought them into ours. We were sharing it with a medical team.

The medical team, many of whom were doctors, quickly surrounded the female trekker. Within minutes they had completed a basic examination and measured her blood-oxygen saturation level. It was 57%! She could die if she wasn't taken down, but it was dark and she couldn't walk. The small room buzzed with discussion, and about 20 minutes later the members of the medical group started assembling a portable hyperbaric chamber they had brought as part of their medical equipment.

The portable hyperbaric chamber was a red cylindrical bag large enough for one person, and created atmospheric pressure equal to about 7,000 feet. They placed the woman in the bag and sealed it, effectively taking her from the current 13,000-foot elevation level to 7,000 feet where the oxygen in the air is about 78%. The idea was to get her through the night so that she could be evacuated by helicopter in the morning. In order to do that, someone outside of the bag had to continuously work the fresh-air foot pump to prevent carbon dioxide build up inside the chamber. With the help of many people, she made it through the night, and the next morning we heard the helicopter come in as we hiked away.

———

The days passed as we worked our way up the valleys. The higher we went, the colder it got but the scenery kept getting more spectacular. We started each morning as a team, but it didn't take long for the group to spread out along the trail. Some of us were comfortable out on our own, and while I enjoyed the company of my teammates, I preferred to hike alone. Sometimes I would stop, captivated by the beautiful valleys surrounded by the snow-capped Himalayan Mountains. The air was crisp and fresh, and filled with the sounds of nature; no machines or human voices to be heard.

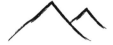

Chapter 6

BASE CAMP: HOME SWEET HOME

On the ninth day of the trek to Base Camp, we left Lobouche (16,100 ft) and headed toward our last stop, Gorak Shep (17,000 ft). We were scheduled to stay two nights at Lobouche but the lodge wasn't the cleanest and no one was having any altitude-related problems, so we decided to move up after the first night. The confines of the lodge caused unavoidable exposure to other people, and by that time, almost everyone in our group had come down with some kind of illness (colds, nausea, fever, and diarrhea). Until that day, I'd been lucky, but now it was my turn. I woke up with a respiratory infection, and thus began my battle to stay on the mountain.

———

At 9:30 AM I walked into Gorak Shep, the last outpost of civilization and our final acclimatization stop before hiking to Base Camp the next day. It was going to be a long day in this very small village, but my spirits were lifted at the sight of a sign boasting of an Internet café. During the trek in, we'd only had Internet access in one other village. If it was working, this would be my last opportunity to use the Internet for a month. The ability to stay connected with my family for one more day was priceless. From this point on, our only form of communication with the outside world would be limited satellite transmissions.

We relaxed in the crowded lodge and ordered some tea and cookies while waiting for the rest of our group to arrive. Scott announced that once everyone had made it to Gorak Shep, he was going to continue on to Base Camp and start getting things set up. I asked him how long the trek would take, and Scott said, "About three hours." I wondered if I should just go with him. Due to my suppressed immune system, I feared, truly feared, spending another day and night in a small lodge exposed to other people and illnesses. Once at Base Camp, we'd all have our own tents and our group would be separated from the other climbing groups. Leaving with Scott was quickly sounding like my best option.

———

Illness was a serious concern for me, and I was already sick with the respiratory infection. Because the Wegener's caused my immune system to attack me, I had to take a strong immunosuppressant medication to intentionally suppress my body's natural defense system. This created two significant problems: it provided an open door for pathogens (infectious agents) to enter my body, and it impeded my body's ability to heal itself. That's why I was literally scared to death of getting sick!

From the time I left home my medications never left my person. Across valleys and up mountains, I carried a backpack of pills. I was a walking pharmacy, and I protected my pills as if they were more precious than gold, because to me, they were. My daily regimen included seven different medications, totaling 16 pills, not counting the antibiotics I was taking for the respiratory infection. At this altitude, if I got any sicker I would have to go back down with the hope of recovering, but if my medications were lost or damaged, my trip would be over.

———

Scott was aware of my special situation and did a great job of not only protecting me, but also everyone else. This was his sixth Everest expedition and he was keenly aware of everything: from a drop of water in a cup to the types of foods offered at the lodges. He rated things according to their potential risk. Drinking from a wet cup washed in untreated local water or eating food that could have spoiled on the way up the valley could make us very, very ill. As a group we worked together to ensure that all water was boiled or purified, all cups and bowls were dry, that everyone washed their hands or used hand-sanitizer before sitting down at a table, and that no one touched another person's eating or drinking dishes. Any infection at this altitude was a major concern; even the smallest scratch had to be closely monitored. Leaving early for Base Camp with Scott was my chance to avoid one more night of potential risk: a sick hiker or a contaminated bowl of soup could send me home.

After a brief discussion, Scott said he would leave the decision up to me. Was I willing to risk altitude sickness to avoid spending another day exposed to potential infections? Leaving early also meant giving up my last chance to send messages home using the Internet. Despite the respiratory infection, I was acclimatizing well and felt strong. But fear directed my thoughts. I was so scared of getting sicker. I had come so far and sacrificed so much. As Scott grabbed his backpack and headed for the door, I followed, and as I crossed the sandy riverbed outside of the village, I thought about my family and whispered messages of love into the wind.

———

The terrain from Gorak Shep to Base Camp started on fairly flat ground, but soon became a series of ups and downs following a rocky ridge of glacial moraine (the debris remnants left behind by receding glaciers of years gone by). As we traversed this seemingly endless mound of boulders, rocks, and sand, I was so focused on my footing that I failed to notice the emerging view. I finally stopped to get my bearings, and as I turned to face the direction of Base Camp, I was struck by my first, full view of Everest.

Powerful first impression: Mt. Everest!

The Nepalese name for Mt. Everest is Sagarmatha: goddess of the sky. And she was! Against the bright blue sky, her dark ominous peak towered over all others. The wind blew the familiar white plume from the summit, and the deadly Khumbu Icefall flowed off her right side. Everest not only emitted an aura of power and danger, but also a beckoning spirituality. Her wondrous presence captivated me. No picture, video, or written word had prepared me for our first face-to-face meeting. Transfixed, I wondered, "Would my insignificant and inconsequential self, be given her blessing and allowed to stand on the top of the world?"

From the distant ridge, Everest Base Camp looked as if someone had thrown handfuls of multicolored marbles across a semi-flat, rocky glacier. Each marble represented a tent and one of those was mine. Excitement flooded my body, washing away the fatigue. I quickened my pace, hopping from rock to rock. I stopped and looked up every few minutes; I couldn't believe that I was almost there, Mt. Everest Base Camp.

We hiked down off of the ridge and started weaving through a maze of boulders and glacial lakes. I tried to keep up with Scott, but I had to focus on my footing. We were now on the glacier and the moraine was mixed with ice. The last thing I wanted was to fall. Rocks, boulders, ice, and more rocks: when were we going to get to camp? As it turned out, we were still about 45 minutes away. Our camp was located at the upper end of Base Camp, close to the Khumbu Icefall.

———

At times there was no clear trail. I knew where I needed to go, but I had yet to learn my way through the maze of lakes and boulders. Whenever I was unsure about which way to go, I looked for the piles of yak dung on the ground, natural trail markers. After working my way around one of the larger glacial lakes, I saw a tower of rocks covered with prayer flags and a sign that said, "Welcome to Mt. Everest Base Camp." There were people everywhere! Some were sitting on the surrounding rocks having lunch, while others were busy taking pictures of everyone and everything. I thought, "What is this place and why are these hikers here?" We hadn't reached Base Camp; there were no tents, only rocks. Scott walked right past the crowd and colorful display, and I followed. Later I was told that the monument was specifically built for Everest Base Camp trekkers who were not scheduled to stay at Base Camp. I thought it was a great idea. It gave the trekkers the feeling that they'd arrived at a destination, but kept them out of the real Base Camp.

As I continued hiking, the colored marbles became a city of tents. There were about 400 climbers and Sherpas, not counting support staff, on the south side of the mountain this season. Base Camp was established on top of an ever-moving glacier, which meant care had to be taken when choosing a specific site to set up individual tents. Scott had sent our Sherpas up weeks earlier to stake out a good location: close to the river and the Khumbu Icefall (our starting point) and hopefully out of avalanche danger.

There were many rituals, rules, and expectations in connection with living at Everest Base Camp. Some were spoken, others assumed, but one tenet was made very clear: you don't enter another group's camp unless invited. This served several purposes. First, it was the defacto home for that group and thus, private. And second, it would, in theory, minimize disease transmission, and everyone knew how serious sickness was at this altitude. In an effort to emphasize this point, many camps posted signs stating, "By Invitation Only" or "Warning, No Entry" or "Keep Out."

Scott quickly navigated these invisible barriers on the way to our camp site, and as we were walking along the river, he suddenly stopped. I looked up and found myself standing just yards away from a large orange, domed tent donning a big sign that read, "MOUNTAIN TRIP 2010 EVEREST EXPEDITION." I was there! This was our base camp and standing right in front of me was a group of stout, smiling men – our Sherpa team. As I took the last few steps up the rocks and entered our camp, I felt like I'd passed through an invisible door and into another reality. And in fact, I had.

I stood there, still wearing my pack. I was overwhelmed with emotions: amazement, happiness, relief, and a childlike sense of wonder. I didn't know what to do or where to go first. Scott was buzzing around from Sherpa to Sherpa giving hugs and handshakes. Many of these men had worked with Scott for years and were like family. After a few minutes, the Sherpas came over and introduced themselves. My head was spinning, as one-by-one they shook my hand and said their names. Many of their names were very similar, and in some cases, were actually the same (Pasang Tendi, Pasang Gombu, Da Wang Chhu, Da Kusang, Pemba Chhotar, Temba – 20 in all). I was both humbled and inspired by these special people. They are nature's mountaineers and I felt honored to be among them.

———

Our camp covered a large area and was comprised of many tents. There were several large tents, some medium ones, and a neat row of smaller, individual tents. We were told which ones were for cooking, storage, sleeping, and toilet facilities. But I was so excited that I had difficulty concentrating; the infamous Khumbu Icefall was just across the small river, and I couldn't take my eyes off of it.

Scott, myself, and three other climbers had arrived at Base Camp a day early, which caused a bit of commotion among the Sherpa staff. They weren't ready for us. As they scrambled to get the final details in order, it became immediately apparent that one Sherpa was in charge: Dawa Sherpa, our Sirdar (head Sherpa). In an effort to stay out of their way, we dropped our packs and went into the large, orange dome, which was our communal area and dining tent.

It was a mountaineer's palace. There were spacious tables covered with tablecloths, comfortable chairs with cushioned seats, and a carpeted floor; things you would expect at home but not at 17,600 feet. The center of the main table was overflowing with all kinds of treats: teas, coffees, drink-mixes, coco, candy, cookies, crackers, chips, nuts, and just about every kind of condiment imaginable. As soon as we were seated, beautiful Chinese thermoses and silver trays piled high with cheeses, meats, fruits, and popcorn followed. It was a feast. As it turned out, we had one of the best, if not *the* best, cooks on the mountain, Serki Sherpa.

After lunch I went outside, looked at the neat row of individual tents, and decided that the third from the end would be my home for the next six weeks. Within minutes of unzipping the tent, two Sherpas delivered my duffle bags from the storage tent. The bags, which contained my mountaineering clothes and equipment, had been sent from Kathmandu ten days earlier, and I was happy to see that everything had arrived. It had taken months of planning to collect the items that I needed for this expedition, and if something was forgotten, broken or lost, it would be almost impossible to replace. For that reason, I had backups for some of the most critical items, such as headlamps, specific climbing gear, and gloves. I could handle not summiting for reasons like weather, health or safety, but if I had to abort summit due to lack of proper equipment, I would be devastated. As I unpacked my duffle bags and organized my tent, I noticed that many of the stuff-sacks were labeled with Larry's name, and tears ran down my cheeks.

———

The fascination of Everest attracts people from all over the world. Some simply want to gaze upon this mighty mountain, while others are there for the challenge of climbing to the top of the world. Unfortunately, this human traffic can have a significant environmental impact. In an effort to minimize the effects, Mountain Trip, along with many other expedition operators, practiced the "Leave No Trace" policy. Whatever was brought up the mountain was taken down. After our visit, all that would remain of us, would be footprints in the snow.

During our six-week stay at Base Camp we needed a power source, and since generators didn't comply with the "Leave No

Trace" policy, solar power was used instead. Within a day of reaching camp, Scott and Bill erected large solar panels, which collected the sunlight needed to charge the storage batteries. Little or no energy could be collected on cloudy, snowy days, so we had to conserve and allocate the camp's stored power according to priorities such as communication radios and the satellite transmission system used for obtaining weather reports.

We also had the ability to send and receive e-mail, but that could only be accomplished using a complex, time-sensitive series of satellite transmissions between Base Camp and Mountain Trip's headquarters in the United States. Only one or two satellite transmissions were sent a day due to limited power and satellite access. So depending on transmission times, it often took days to send a message and receive a reply. But the ability to have even limited contact with home was an amazing luxury, and we had to take care not to abuse it.

In an effort to keep the system from overloading, we were each assigned a special e-mail address and asked to limit the number of people who contacted us. Our e-mail access may have been limited, but for me, any communication with home was a gift.

Before leaving, I gave my Everest e-mail address to Larry, Teshia, and two media people: Rob Struass, a producer for Southern California Public Radio, who was arranging a series of satellite phone interviews with Alex Cohen of *All Things Considered*; and Mary-Rose Abraham, an ABC television reporter who was covering the story for *World News* with Diane Sawyer. While the media coverage was an important part of my effort to raise rare disease awareness, it was my ability to communicate with home that helped me battle my biggest enemy, loneliness.

We also had access to two satellite phones. These phones worked fairly well considering we were in a valley surrounded by the world's tallest mountains. Although I had practiced in Kathmandu, this type of phone was new to me and using it at

17,600 feet took patience. First, I had to locate the satellite, and then I would attempt to connect to it. Each time a connection failed, I'd have to move to a slightly different location and try again. On average, it took five attempts to get a connection. Once connected to the satellite, I could dial the number I was trying to reach, and with a little luck, the call would go through. And if the person answered, the trick became to stay within the satellite's range or the call would disconnect and I would have to start all over again. Sometimes, I would get disconnected three or four times trying to make a single call. And because of the 12 hour and 45 minute time difference with home, calls had to be made in the morning or at night. This meant standing outside in the finger-numbing cold, dialing a small phone.

———

One of the most important and difficult aspects of living at altitude is eating. Loss of appetite is common at high altitude and having the proper kind and quantity of food can make or break someone's ability to climb. Eating was easiest at Base Camp. We had access to many types of food and our Base Camp cook, Serki, created amazing meals. But higher up, the loss of appetite combined with limited food choices made eating more difficult and at times, impossible.

On rest days, I needed to eat at least 2,500 calories to maintain my strength and weight. On climbing days, I needed to eat at least twice as much in an effort to keep my body fueled. Unfortunately, there were days when I couldn't even eat a quarter of the calories required, and when that happened, my body resorted to using itself for fuel. Everyone's body has extra stored fuel in the form of fat, but the body will also start burning muscles, and I needed my muscles to climb. So I ate as much and as often as I could, but I was fighting a losing battle.

Eating at altitude was, and still is, my biggest problem. But knowledge is power, and during my training climbs, I learned what foods I could eat under those conditions, and I planned accordingly. I brought these foods from home and saved them for the days when I couldn't eat anything else. I had prepackaged cheese and crackers, trail mix, soup mixes, and candy bars. As an experiment, I brought a can of Kraft Cheez Whiz, and to my surprise and delight it didn't explode and worked fine (when it wasn't frozen). And I discovered what I called "my magic food" that I saved for dinner the night before the summit.

I also had an additional issue when it came to eating – timing. The medication I take to control the Wegener's has to be taken twice a day and on an empty stomach. This means that I can't eat two hours before or one hour after taking it. So, every day I needed two, three-hour fasting windows in order to take my pills. This created such a conflict. I was supposed to eat as much as I could all of the time, but I couldn't eat for three hours each morning and three hours each evening. And, since I couldn't lie down after ingesting the medication, because it can cause severe esophageal damage, I couldn't take it before or during sleep time. So I had to time my eating around the medication schedule, and the higher we went, the more difficult that got.

On a normal day when breakfast was around 7:30 AM, I would take my medication at about 6 AM. It was still too cold to go outside, so I would try to occupy myself by doing things inside my tent. Later in the day, I would have to skip the afternoon snack, so that I could take my second round of medication and still be able to eat dinner at about 7 PM. So while waiting to eat, I would write in my journal, play cards if someone was around, or more often than not, I would just sit and think.

———

To climb Everest from the south side requires going through the dangerous, ever-moving Khumbu Icefall. More lives have been lost there than on any other part of the mountain. At the beginning of each climbing season, a team of specialized Sherpas called the Icefall Doctors determines the safest route through the icefall, and fixes ropes and aluminum ladders up the 2,000-foot river of flowing ice. Without the work of the Icefall Doctors, climbing through the icefall would be next to impossible.

While the Icefall Doctors work on the route through the icefall, climbing operators meet to discuss who, how, and when the remainder of the mountain will be fixed with rope. In recent years, climbing companies and guides combine resources in a collaborative effort to fix a line all the way to the summit. Groups donate equipment such as ropes and anchors, manpower in the form of Sherpas, and/or money to pay for expenses. In the end, it becomes everyone's safety line.

By the time we arrived at Base Camp, the Icefall Doctors had completed the route. But our Puja blessing ceremony needed to be held before the Sherpas would enter the icefall. According to their beliefs, the mountains are the domain of the gods and goddesses. No one may step on Everest's sacred slopes without first asking Sagarmatha, goddess of the sky, for her permission and blessing for safe passage.

The date of the Puja ceremony is based on the Sherpa calendar. We arrived at base camp on April 16th and according to Dawa Sherpa, our Lama, the best day for our Puja was April 21st. This meant at least a six-day delay before the equipment and supplies for our higher camps could be carried up. Scott was concerned that the delay would put us behind schedule, but it was nonnegotiable. The Lama wouldn't hold the Puja sooner, and the Sherpas refused to climb until after the ceremony.

So we waited and watched as the preparations began. First the chorten, a tall stone alter, was built. While that was happening, our head cook, Serki, was so busy in the kitchen tent that we hardly saw him. I wasn't sure what was going on, but the camp buzzed with activity. I felt the excitement in the air.

————

By the time I crawled out of my tent on the day of the Puja, the chorten was already beautifully decorated with the special cakes and pastries that Serki had made. We ate a quick breakfast while the Sherpas made the final preparations. Then we were asked to place our ice axes, crampons, and harnesses along one side of the chorten, as our climbing gear would also be blessed during the ceremony. The three Lamas were seated facing the chorten, their prayer books on a table in front of them, and everyone in camp sitting around them. The incense was lit and the Puja began.

————

The Puja was an interesting and complex event that lasted over five hours. Prayers were read, offerings of food and drink were made, and rituals observed. During the Puja, each climber, including myself, received a special necklace meant to keep us safe. When I leant forward to accept mine, Dawa Lama tied the blessing necklace around my neck, and I didn't remove it until I was safely at home.

Although I didn't understand the "why" of certain rituals, I couldn't help but get swept-up by their spiritual energy. Once the prayers were read and the necklaces received, the ceremony transformed into a more playful event. It started with everyone taking flour and throwing it three times into the air. Then the Sherpas came around, and with both hands full of flour, smeared it across everyone's cheeks. Next, silver trays containing all types of food and drink were carried among us. The number three is very special and we had to take three of everything: three pieces of food and three drinks of whatever.

The final event of the Puja was breathtaking. I stood watching as a flag pole was raised from the center of the chorten; and suddenly the sky was filled with the blue, white, red, green, and yellow colors of prayer flags. They were lifted high in the air and stretched for hundreds of feet in every direction. Our entire camp was now held within their colorful embrace. As the wind blew over the prayer flags, each flutter released unspoken prayers and blessings into the wind.

The Puja Ceremony.

For six weeks I lived at 17,600 feet or higher, in a tent, on an ever-moving glacier, a few hundred yards away from the dangerous Khumbu Icefall. Each morning I woke up, looked up at Mt. Everest, and wondered, "How is she feeling today?" Each night when I went to bed, I felt her power running through me, and I would ask her to keep us safe.

Standing in front of our individual tents at Base Camp with the Khumbu Icefall in the background. (Photo by Jona-Marie Price)

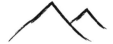

Chapter 7

SOLUS

We arrived at Base Camp as a group of 12: five Base Camp trekkers (all females), five Everest climbers, and two Everest guides. One of the trekkers, Jona-Marie, was scheduled to climb the nearby Lobuche Peak (20,100 ft) in preparation for climbing Everest next season. It was wonderful to have the ladies with us for those first few days. They filled Base Camp with their carefree energy and laughter. But our goals were different and we soon had to say goodbye. The trekkers left for their hike back down the valley while Jona-Marie headed off to the Lobuche Peak base camp. A few days later, we received word that the ladies were in Kathmandu waiting to fly home and that Jona-Marie had made her summit.

———

We were now seven. Scott was the expedition leader, an amazing high altitude guide, and already a four-time Everest summiter. Bill was the co-owner of Mountain Trip International, and while this was his first Everest climb, he was also an extremely experienced high-altitude guide. These men had spent their lives learning the secrets of the mountains, the snow, the ice, and the weather; and safety was always their first priority.

My climbing team consisted of three females and two males, which was unusual since most summit teams were predominantly male: Ania, a Polish woman who currently lived and worked in London; Vivian, an Irishman who lived and worked in New York; and Paul and Denise, a married couple from Newport Beach, California. All four of my teammates were climbing the Seven Summits (the highest mountain on each of the seven continents), and Everest was their last challenge. If they made it to the summit; Ania, Vivian, Paul, and Denise would become members of the Seven Summits Club, an impressive accomplishment.

And then there was me, a misfit of sorts. At age 51, I was 12-years older than the next oldest climber, and I was the least experienced of the group, having only three years of climbing under my belt (minus the year I lost from disease complications and two leg surgeries). I had only reached two of the Seven Summits, but climbing the Seven Summits had never been my goal. For me, climbing other mountains was training for the world's highest summit – Everest.

———

Life at Base Camp evolved into a simple routine: breakfast at 7:30 AM, lunch at 1:30 PM, and dinner at 7 PM. The rest of the day was filled with time. Sure, there was laundry to wash, gear to pack or unpack, half-day hikes up nearby mountains, journals to write, and maybe a predinner card game, but mostly there was just time.

I was used to traveling to unknown places with unknown people, but I always had Larry. Now, I didn't. Every day, almost without exception, my thoughts were of home. I knew that dealing with the separation and loneliness would be the hardest part, and it was.

My journal entries from the first few days at Base Camp:

Saturday, April 17th

I slept ok. The rest of the team arrived today. Did laundry. Waiting to check e-mail and sat phone. I have had no contact with Larry for days. I am going to call Larry later. ☺

Sunday, April 18th

Had a great call with Larry last night. Helped my spirits! Today we rested. I sorted gear. Snowed most of the afternoon. Watched an avalanche – was amazing.

Monday, April 19th

I have been gone for 18 days. 6 weeks to go. ☹ *Trekking group left today. We did ladder training – too fun! Took a towelette bath and have warm clothes on. It is about 5:30 PM. Gets very cold when sun goes down. Another big avalanche this morning. Power blast got our tents. I love you Larry!*

Tuesday, April 20th

Had a headache this morning after hiking to 18,400 ft. Took a hot shower today – first in a week! Got a nice e-mail from Larry ☺ *and I need Teshia's e-mail address (she changed it). Packing for five days up high. I think about home and Larry all the time. Teshia has her boyfriend.* ☺

Wednesday, April 21st

We had our Puja ceremony today. We were supposed to leave for Camp 1 in the morning but it has been delayed one day. Good thing – I was sick after dinner last night. ☹ *Hope this thing goes away!*

> ## *Thursday, April 22ⁿᵈ*
>
> *Still sick this morning but did eat an egg. Then we went up the Khumbu Icefall and practiced ladders. That was great but I was weak from being sick. Could not eat much lunch but took a shower! Repacked my pack so it is a little lighter. ☺ Just hope I did not leave out too much. Five days up high – I will find out. Think of Larry all the time. I will call him from Camp 2. ☺ We leave Base Camp at 5 AM.*

———

We were leaving for our first rotation to Camp 2 in the morning, and while I had finished my antibiotic medication days ago, my respiratory infection was no better. I was constantly coughing. That evening before dinner, Scott, Bill, and some other teammates, donated all types of cough drops for me to take. We would be up there for five nights, and our tents would only be a few yards apart. While my coughing made me miserable, it was almost as bad for everyone who had to listen to it. They were, however, all very gracious and no one complained, at least not directly to me.

———

The days on the mountain were a time of personal hardship and personal growth. We were a team of seven though I felt alone among others. In my mind I had known this would happen, but my heart didn't understand. I knew I was mentally tough, but was I tough enough to get through the terrible loneliness? As the days and weeks passed, it was my stubborn determination to climb the mountain that anchored me.

I learned to endure the physical and emotional suffering. Pushing myself into the unknown revealed an inner strength, a power, that I had never felt before. From this, I realized that reaching the summit of self-awareness was worth much more than reaching the summit of Mt. Everest.

My own empowerment also gave me the insight to understand those who found Everest too much to bear. I watched, not in judgment, but in understanding, as they packed their bags and left the mountain. I was lucky. I had found the key to open the door of enigmatic uncertainty, and I stepped through, powerful and sure.

Climbing Mt. Everest was my chance to show people the importance of reaching for their dreams. I've always believed that life isn't about waiting for the storm to pass; it's about learning to dance in the rain. I would take it one day at a time, but in my soul I knew that I had the spirit to do this, and when the time came, I would look up, get the full picture, check my harness, clip onto the rope, and go. I had a mountain to climb – if only *10-feet-at-a-time*.

Map of south side climbing routes and camp locations. Courtesy of Alan Arnette, who summited on May 21, 2011, as part of his "7 Summits for Alzheimer's: Memories are Everything" quest. For more go to www.alanarnette.com

Chapter 8

ROPES AND LADDERS

As the Sherpas carried loads of supplies up to the higher camps, we trained and acclimatized lower on the mountain. Acclimatizing for the extreme altitude of Everest required a repeating cycle of climbing and waiting. We were scheduled for two, five-night rotations up the mountain before going for the summit. On the first rotation we would climb to Camp 1 and Camp 2, and then come back down to Base Camp. After resting for a few days, we would complete our second rotation by returning to Camp 2, and continuing up to Camp 3, before again heading back to Base Camp. While the process was necessary, it also required us to climb the dangerous Khumbu Icefall six times, each exponentially increasing the odds of an accident.

———

We left Base Camp for our first rotation at 5 AM on April 23rd. With our headlamps shining on the icy ground, we stepped into the darkness and headed for the Khumbu Icefall. I was weak and still sick, but that didn't matter; it was time to go and I had to focus. For the next four hours I would be climbing through the most deadly section of the mountain – over 1.5 miles and 2,000 vertical feet up a tangled, moving mass of giant ice blocks (seracs) and bottomless crevasses. Crossing the icefall takes speed, strength, concentration, and luck. There are many bodies locked within the Khumbu's icy hold and I had no intention of joining them.

———

The scraping of my crampons on the ice was the only sound in the cold, still air. My teammates were somewhere on the mountain, either ahead or behind. Occasionally, I'd see the flicker of a headlamp but then it would disappear. As I got further away from Base Camp, a mysterious excitement crept over me, luring me further into the icy blackness.

As I made my way onto the icefall, I kept looking up into the darkness. I sensed the danger ahead, even though I couldn't see it. Weeks earlier, the Icefall Doctors had anchored a rope up through the icefall, and using the light from my headlamp, I located it and clipped onto it with a metal carabineer that, by way of a nylon leash, was tied to my harness. In theory, if I fell I would stay attached to the rope, and at some point it would stop me, allowing for either self-recovery or if necessary and possible, a rescue.

———

The rope was both friend and foe. It provided a measure of safety and guidance, but because it was anchored to a constantly moving, shifting, and twisting flow of ice, it was also unreliable. This was especially dangerous in the darkness because it could be misleading. In one location, the rope crossed a semi-frozen, glacial lake and following it could be a fatal mistake. In other areas, it completely disappeared into a mass of collapsed ice. Bottom line: the rope was only an aid.

———

The sky began to lighten after a few hours of climbing, and with the light of day came the harsh reality of the beautiful but deadly icefall. The darkness had allowed me to climb blissfully blind to my extended surroundings, but now I could see the depth of the crevasses, the sheerness of the walls, and the size of the overhanging seracs just waiting to fall. With each passing hour, the air got warmer and the icefall less stable. It became a race against the sun as a falling serac, avalanche, or collapse would be almost impossible to escape.

The sun also unveiled the Khumbu's stunning beauty. It was literally and figuratively breathtaking. I had seen photographs and read stories, but no pictures or words had come close to depicting the feeling of standing amidst all of this indescribable beauty. Hour after hour I continued up through a seemingly endless gauntlet of ever-changing terrain. Speed and adaptability were critical as each move revealed a different challenge. I literally climbed the icefall *10-feet-at-a-time*. Clipped onto the rope, I would traverse a narrow ledge that would end at a wall. I'd climb up the wall, only to find an ice bridge at the top. I'd cross the bridge, and then come to a crevasse. I jumped the smaller crevasses, but had to use the ladders to walk across, up, or down the larger ones.

Climbing through the Khumbu Icefall.
(Photo by Bill Allen)

———

Crossing the ladders was interesting to say the least. Each day as the ice moved, so did the ladders. Speed was essential, but so was safety. I had to carefully assess each ladder's stability before stepping onto it. Both the movement of the icefall and other climbers crossing the ladders caused a variety of dangerous changes: anchors loosened or came completely out, the safety rope was compromised, or the ice supporting the ladder collapsed without warning. If I was lucky, there would be someone ahead of me, and I'd watch how the ladder reacted as they crossed it. But most of the time no one was within view, so I just stepped onto it.

Some of the ladders would twist sideways as soon as I stepped onto them. When that happened I used myself as a counterbalance, leaning the other way as I scrambled across. Other ladders weren't quite long enough to span the whole crevasse, and would have additional anchors attached to them in an attempt to limit how far they would drop (a few inches or a few feet) when a climber stepped onto them. And if two or more ladders were tied together, crossing became even trickier.

In order to cross a ladder, I had to place my foot so that it touched two rungs with my toes on one, and my heel on another, so that the tips of both the front and rear crampon-points would catch the rungs with every step. Vision aside, I had another problem, the actual size of my foot. Even with my big boots and crampons, my foot was almost too small to reach between the rungs. One misplaced tip and I might fall into the crevasse. People often ask me if I ever looked down into the crevasse while crossing ladders, and I reply, "I didn't want to look but I had to. I focused on my feet and the ladder while trying not to see what was below." I couldn't care about what was down there. I just had to get across.

Usually only one climber was on a ladder at a time, and most ladders had an anchored side-rope to help the climber balance. Stability was critical over large crevasses, especially where two or more ladders had been roped together. I cannot explain what it was like to be on a twisting, wobbly ladder, straddling a gaping, bottomless crack in the ice, and being forced to constantly look down in order to carefully move my feet and crampons from one uneven rung to the next. Many times my tips wouldn't quite reach the next rung and I would have to do a little hop dance, hoping I didn't slip.

There were 40 or so ladders in the icefall, and each had its own personality. Some were short and well-anchored while others were less stable or in more dangerous locations. Some ladders would bounce, usually while I was right in the middle of them, and if it was a windy day, well, then it got really thrilling. The excitement of ladder-crossing never diminished, but after a while I was able to categorize each one: "easy," "okay," "short and twisty," "long but stable," and "oh my gosh – not that one!"

———

The last few hundred feet up the icefall was both spectacular and extremely dangerous. By the time we reached that point, the sun had been warming the ice for hours. We hurried across ladder after ladder, going up and down, over and across ice pinnacles, crevasses, and seracs. When there was no ladder, we jumped. Time was critical. As I stood waiting to cross one of the more dangerous ladders, I watched two minor icefall-collapses off to my left. They were considered "minor" because no one was on or under them at the time.

Waiting for my turn to cross a ladder in the upper part of the Khumbu Icefall. (Photo by Bill Allen)

There were two routes up to the top of the icefall. One included a 60 or 70 foot ice wall that had multiple connecting ladders anchored up its face. The other was a very steep, narrow ledge with a vertical climb at the top. We chose the ledge over the ladders, but before I could take my first step, I heard a loud crack under my feet. As I clipped onto the rope, I felt the ice under me move. I quickly stepped onto the ledge.

———

When I pulled myself over the lip of the ice wall, it was like emerging into another world. An enormous valley of snow and ice surrounded by the world's tallest mountains: Everest was on my left, Nuptse on my right, and Lhotse was straight ahead. In all my life, I'd never seen such beauty or felt such power.

The terrain was relatively level at the top of the icefall, giving me my first view of the Western Cwm (pronounced coom). I slowly walked over to where Scott and Vivian were sitting, and took off my pack. It was our first break since leaving Base Camp over four hours before, but this was no place to stay. We were still in a very dangerous area. Once the team regrouped, we were off to our stop for the night – Camp 1 at 19,500 feet.

———

We spent one night at Camp 1, and then headed up the Western Cwm toward Camp 2 at 21,600 feet. The Western Cwm is a large, glacial valley. At first glance, its gradual slopes were a welcome sight, but it didn't take long to realize that it was fraught with danger. The valley was filled with crevasses and hidden snow bridges. The weather was also a constant concern. This was our first time up the Western Cwm and it was a cold, windy day; little did I know that I would later dream of such pleasant conditions.

During the seemingly endless climb through the Western Cwm, I was so focused on getting to Camp 2 that I never
really saw my surroundings. Hour after hour, I concentrated
on putting one foot in front of the other. Our campsite was at
the upper end of Camp 2, closer to the Lhotse Face and along
the south-west face of Everest. This meant that even after I
got to Camp 2, I still had a half-hour more to go before reaching our camp. I finally arrived, and even though it felt like it
had taken all day, it was only late morning. I threw my pack
into my tent and looked around. I was awestruck by the view.
Only nature could make something so magical. I was instantly
re-energized, euphoric that I had actually made it to Camp 2,
but so had my cough. I had now been sick for eight days, and at
this altitude, there was no hope of getting better, only worse.

We stayed at Camp 2 for four nights to acclimatize, but life
was harsh at 21,600 feet. The effects of the altitude caused
everything to be more difficult. Here, each breath I took only
contained 45% of the amount of oxygen as compared to air at
sea level. I would get winded just putting on my boots and
walking 15 feet to the dining tent. And if I had to use the toilet
tent up over the hill, well, that could wait.

Simple luxuries in this hostile environment really helped
morale. We were fortunate to have a table and three-legged
stools in our dining tent. It was fantastic to be able to sit without being scrunched up on the tent floor, especially when trying to eat. And eating was becoming increasingly problematic
for me. I was experiencing the loss-of-appetite side effect that
comes with high altitude; just looking at food made me nauseous. And to complicate matters, I had to take many of my
medications with food, but the one that controlled my disease
had to be taken on a completely empty stomach. Every day,
I needed those two, three-hour windows of not eating while

trying to eat every other chance I got – it was crazy! But I was prepared. I had my special foods from home, hoping they would entice me to eat. On this rotation I had brought cheese and crackers, animal cookies, and rice crispy treats. I needed the fuel to continue to climb, and I needed the medication to keep my disease in check. Eating became a constant battle between my body and my brain.

Mind-numbing boredom was another ever-present menace. In order for our bodies to make the physiology changes needed to go higher up the mountain, we had to spend many days at extreme altitude. The days were filled with hours and the hours were filled with minutes. It was all time, just empty time. Mostly we stayed in our tents where lethargy quickly set in. I knew it was important not to fall victim to inactivity, and I made a conscious effort to get out of my tent and walk around, but before long, I would find myself right back in my tent. My lack of motivation combined with the wind, the cold, and the snow caused a self-imposed sequester. I spent hour after hour alone in my tent just staring at its orange walls.

———

On the third day at Camp 2, I went for a short hike and met up with two of my teammates. As we stood talking and admiring the view, someone asked, "Is that a body over there?" It was. We hiked back to our tents and never talked about it again, not even amongst ourselves. Later, as we were leaving Base Camp and heading for home, we were told that the body was a climber from the previous season. It's expensive and dangerous to get bodies down from that altitude. Thus, the mountain becomes the final resting place for many who perish up high.

———

The next morning we hiked to the base of the Lhotse Face. I stood looking up the 3,700-foot, blue ice wall with the black pyramid-like summit of Everest off to its left. It was an awesome site! I could see that it was going to be a challenging climb. So far this season there had been only one death on the south side of Everest, and it had occurred on the Lhotse Face.

The elevation at the base of the Lhotse Face matched my personal climbing-height record; and every step up from here would take me higher than I'd ever climbed. I asked Scott to take a picture of me holding the NORD banner with Everest's summit in the background, just in case something happened and this was as high as I would get. To have Wegener's and climb to over 22,000 feet was, by itself, an amazing accomplishment. The excitement was building in me and I felt ready for the challenge, but this would not be the day. We weren't going any higher, so after having some snacks, we headed back down to Camp 2.

*Me holding NORD banner at the base of the Lhotse
Face with Everest in the background.
(Photo by Scott Woolums)*

———

We left Camp 2 at 4 AM on April 28th, and climbed down through the Western Cwm, the Khumbu Icefall, and back to Base Camp. We had completed our first 5-day rotation up the mountain. It had been the most difficult and dangerous climbing I had ever done. I stepped out of the icefall with a deeper, more comprehensive sense of awareness and understanding of the extraordinary physical demands and psychological strength needed to survive on a mountain like Everest. Yes, I knew that each day, and each higher camp would bring new challenges and unimagined dangers, but I truly believed that I would stand on the top of this mountain. She'd held out her hand, and I had accepted.

———

As I walked into camp and headed toward my tent, I noticed that all of our tents had shifted while we were gone. They were closer together, and the rocks and boulders that had served as our front porches had receded. This became a standing joke: "Hey, your property value is going down" or "where did your yard go?" The glacier was melting.

Once at my tent, I dropped my pack, removed my crampons and harness, and pulled off my big boots. I couldn't wait to free my feet from the bonds of those mammoth boots, and peel off the socks that I'd been wearing for the last five days. I sat at the opening of my tent for several minutes wriggling my toes in the cold, fresh air. It was great to be back to the relative luxuries of Base Camp. Now, what I wanted most was to be clean. I didn't even wait for the water to be warmed up. I just grabbed the bucket of cold water, and headed for the shower tent.

———

After dinner, I called Larry on the sat phone. I tried to call him each time we crossed the Khumbu Icefall so he'd know that I had made it safely across. I can't imagine what it must've been like for him so far away, so unaware. That night it was unusually difficult to get the satellite connection. After about 15 minutes of walking around camp, searching for a signal, I finally heard Larry's voice on the phone. That second, while standing in the biting cold of the Everest evening, I was transported home. It was as if he was right next to me. In a calm and relaxed voice, he told me about his day. The call lasted only minutes, but my smile lasted for days.

―――――

As part of my rare disease awareness campaign, I posted updates on my blog and did several satellite phone interviews with NPR radio host Alex Cohen of *All Things Considered*. I had limited communication with the outside world and I understood the potential effect my words could have on those so far away. In a conscious effort to provide only positive or factual information, I purposefully omitted details that might cause people, especially my family, to worry.

Everest has a dark side. Her beauty and wonder must not distract from the ever-present danger. The accidents and deaths that occurred on Everest were, if possible, kept quiet. We were rarely told about things that happened on the mountain. If directly involved, we were asked to stay silent. If we heard something, we were reminded that rumors only caused more problems in such a remote location where facts were almost impossible to verify. We were advised to keep to ourselves and not to talk or post about such things.

Chapter 9

CRAZY BECOMES THE NORM

For two nights, we rested in the thick air of Base Camp waiting for our next five-day rotation up the mountain. I was packed and ready to go, but my coughing was getting worse. I coughed all day and all night, and there was nothing I could do to stop it. The only time I didn't cough was while climbing. If I stopped moving, even for a few seconds, the coughing started up, weird. I'd heard stories about climbers whose coughing became so violent that it broke their ribs. The only way my condition was going to improve was if I went down the mountain, but I couldn't. The next rotation was just hours away.

———

We left Base Camp for our second rotation at 4 AM on May 1st. While it was our third climb through the Khumbu Icefall, each trip up was different. The icefall changed by the hour and as it got later in the season, the air got warmer, and the icefall became even more dangerous. Just two days before, there had been two large collapses in the upper part of the icefall. Thankfully no one was hurt, but parts of the route we used on the first rotation were now buried under tons of ice.

I recognized most of the lower icefall, but about three hours into the climb, the route abruptly changed. The collapse had completely altered this section. It was now an even steeper torrent of ice and seracs. Ladders had been swept away, and in places, the collapse had filled in crevasses, but that didn't mean they were safe to cross.

I cannot say if the icefall was more treacherous now, however, it did seem to be a more strenuous climb the second time. But it's hard to know if the climbing was more difficult or if I was just weaker. The longer we stayed at these extreme altitudes, the more our bodies deteriorated. We were literally wasting away.

———

Once up the icefall we rested for a few minutes at Camp 1 before heading onto the Western Cwm. Unlike the first rotation with its cold windy weather, crossing the Western Cwm this time was like walking into an oven turned on high. As I made my way up the valley, the heat became stifling. Without a breath of wind to move the air or a cloud in the sky, the sun's rays reflected up off of every snowy, icy surface and directly onto me; it was blazing white heat from every direction. I stopped, drank some water, and removed every layer of clothing I could, but the temperature kept rising. I could see Camp 2, like a distant mirage, though it was still hours away. I slowed my pace and continued on.

I have no idea how long it took, but I arrived at Camp 2 in time for lunch, and by nightfall a storm had moved in. We were scheduled to stay five nights at 21,600 feet. Someone said it was easier the second time up, but so far it was worse.

———

The storm lasted for days, but the bad weather hadn't yet interfered with our schedule. We had to stay at this altitude in order for our bodies to adjust, and weather permitting, we'd eventually leave to climb up the Lhotse Face to Camp 3. In the meantime, there was nothing to do but wait.

During these stormy days and nights, I spent most of the time in my tent listening to the howling wind. At times, I put on every layer of clothing I had and made the 15-foot journey to the dining tent, and that's when I truly appreciated the table and three-legged stools. It was hard enough to eat and breathe at this altitude without having a compressed diaphragm and aching back. Usually by late afternoon, sheer boredom would drive others from their seclusion and into the dining tent. It was only a matter of time before three people came in which meant the beginning of a card game. Funny how difficult keeping score was at almost 22,000 feet.

We usually stayed in the dining tent long enough to eat dinner, but the evening cold would drive us back to our individual tents. I always circled my tent before entering, checking all the lines and anchors, making them as secure as possible for the night. The wind would take advantage of a loose line, and I didn't want to go out in the cold trying to fix my tent before the wind damaged it. How cold was it? Cold!

With the exception of my ice ax and crampons, I kept all of my gear inside my tent. At night I donned every layer of clothing I had and crawled into my sleeping bag, which also housed everything that I didn't want to freeze: boot liners, gloves, water bottles, cameras, medications, and food. The "stuff" usually took up about a third of my bag. Sequestered by the cold, I would snuggle in for the long, lonely wait until sunrise.

———

For the most part, our camp weathered the storm with the exception of the toilet tent. Being up over the hill and in a more exposed area, it didn't survive the days and nights of high winds. Once the storm subsided, it was repaired as best as possible. In the meantime, I had my port-a-potty effects inside my tent and they served me well. Practice makes perfect, and I got very skilled at using my indoor facilities. There was no way I was going out into that storm and expect to be able to ... Nope, it wasn't happening. A bottle and a zip-lock bag worked nicely.

———

We were lucky and on the third morning the weather cleared, and we left for Camp 3 at 5 AM. It turned out to be a wonderful, windless, sunny day: perfect conditions for climbing the blue ice wall of the Lhotse Face. It took about 45 minutes to reach its base, and after a short break, we started up. The first section was quite challenging. It was steep, blue ice and we had to jump over and up crevasse-like gaps while simultaneously trying to anchor ourselves by kicking our crampon-tips into the steely ice when we landed. It was during times like these that I most appreciated my ability to direct my brain to pure analytical thinking. This allowed me to concentrate on the mechanics of the situation and leave the emotions behind, almost.

By now, this crazy, dangerous type of climbing was becoming the norm. It had taken guts and strength to climb the base-wall, and once up, I stared at the thousands of feet of sheer, vertical blue ice that I would be climbing for the next several hours. Now more than ever, I had to focus on safety. If I came unclipped from the rope on the Lhotse Face, I would fall to my death.

It took hours of strenuous climbing up that ice-wall to reach the area that would serve as Camp 3, and for me, the last hour was the most difficult. At this altitude, each breath of air only contained 42% of the normal amount of oxygen. Sometimes I took four or five breaths between each step. I could see where I needed to go, and it wasn't that far, but why couldn't I get there? I just kept moving, *10-feet-at-a-time*, and finally reached the rest of the group. Still attached to the safety line, I used my crampons to kick a small platform out of the ice and then sat down to rest. As tired as I was, it felt amazing to be at almost 24,000 feet! Very few people have been to this height, and I was now one of them. We stayed awhile enjoying the view and having some snacks before we headed back down to Camp 2 for the night.

———

I posted this blog entry via satellite transmission from Camp 2 the following day:

My Family

Yesterday we went to Camp 3 and today we are resting at Camp 2. I have been gone for five weeks now and I am missing my family a great deal.

I also posted a picture of myself standing outside at Camp 2 holding two photos: one of my husband and one of my daughter. I kept those pictures on me whenever I was climbing, so they would always be with me.

*Teammate Vivian Rigney was kind enough to
take this picture of me and my family.*

———

We left Camp 2 at 4 AM on May 6th, and went down through
the Khumbu Icefall to Base Camp. We had completed the second rotation. The next time we would cross the icefall would
be on our way to the summit. It was now a waiting game. We
needed rest and a five-day weather window in order to try for
the summit. Later that night I called Larry on the satellite
phone to tell him I was safely back at Base Camp.

———

Tomorrow we would leave and hike down to the Snow Lion Lodge at Dingboche (13,500 ft). With two rotations completed we had earned a vacation; not a typical vacation but a break from life at Base Camp and the extremes of Everest. We were scheduled to spend four nights in the more oxygen-rich air of the lower valley while waiting for our summit window to open. After so long at such high altitude, our bodies needed to rest and recover. It was a chance for cuts and sores to heal, and maybe, just maybe, for my cough to go away too.

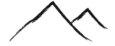

Chapter 10

MOTHER'S DAY IN DINGBOCHE

As on any big-mountain expedition, organization, coordination, and cooperation were paramount to a safe and successful trip. And the harsh, remote environment imposed a myriad of restrictions. While this was an accepted aspect of climbing, Everest was different. Most climbs were completed within weeks not months.

———

On the morning of May 7th I waved to our Sherpas as I walked away from Base Camp and headed down the valley to Dingboche. I knew the way, and felt completely comfortable hiking alone. In fact, I preferred it. It had been over five weeks since I'd left home, and during this time my loneliness had evolved into a sense of serene self-confidence. But my self-imposed captivity created a desperate need to escape the mountain in order to rejuvenate both my body and soul.

On the way down, I occasionally passed Ania or she passed me, but for the most part, we hiked alone. After a few hours, I began to feel different. I didn't know what it was at first, but as I continued on down the valley, I realized that what I felt was "freedom." I was "free" to decide when to stop for a break, which trail to take, or whether to have tea at a village or just keep going. I was no longer controlled by the restrictions of the camp or the mountain. Until that moment, I hadn't realized just how much control I had given up, but now I was free to make my own decisions, if only for a few days.

———

Overall, I believe that people who come to climb Everest are assertive, independent, strong-willed, self-directed individuals who make their own way through their days and their lives, and I was no exception. In preparation for this trip, I had meticulously researched every aspect, every possibility – even death. But in my wildest dreams of what Everest might bring (and I had some pretty wild dreams), the loss of control over even the smallest aspects of my daily life never entered my mind.

The acquiescence of control was directed by the situation or circumstance, and the transformation was so subtle that I didn't recognize it. In retrospect, it had started the minute I left home, and as the days turned into weeks, and the world around me became more unfamiliar and remote, my ability to make decisions dissolved into "what was" or "what must be." I first became aware of that at mealtime. At home I made what I wanted to eat. In Kathmandu I chose from a wide variety of restaurants. On the trek up to Base Camp I selected from the lodge's menu, but once at Base Camp, the meals were set. Mountain Trip spared no expense to provide us with an amazing assortment of foods, but the options were controlled by availability, storage, and the limitations of high-altitude cooking. Thankfully, we had a fantastic cook. Serki could use one food item and create a dozen different dishes. But over time, the food became the same and I had to force myself to eat. There was no choice.

———

My words should not be mistaken for self-pity or complaint. I'm simply describing my observation of an unexpected psychological manifestation. It was to become one of many introspective enlightenments that I would experience during the course of this adventure. Exploring life, especially at its extremes, invariably reveals one's true nature.

I was on Everest of my own accord, and free to leave at any time. I had, in fact, watched as others packed their bags and left. They had their reasons, but for me there was never a single day, a single moment, that I felt like I couldn't go on. I was following my dream to climb to the top of the world. I was going to summit this mountain.

––––

Mingma Sherpa managed the Snow Lion Lodge as if it were named after her personality. She was a female Sherpa with the cunning of a lion and the strength of a yak. I had broken through her gruff exterior during our initial stay at the lodge on the way up to Base Camp almost a month earlier. She had a great sense of humor and was also a worthy opponent at cards.

As soon as Ania and I came through the door, Mingma walked over and gave us both a big hug. She understood the ravages of life up high and quickly showed us to our rooms so we could relax. My small plywood-walled room was a wonderful change from weeks in a tent. Here I had a window, nails on which to hang clothes, and a padded platform where I could sit and sleep. I unpacked the items I had carried down. There wasn't much, just the basic necessities: medication, tooth brush, soap, socks, camera, headlamp, an extra set of clothes, my journal, and a sleeping bag. I carefully organized my small room, and then sat on the bunk looking out the window. After living for so long with so little, it felt odd to be back in civilization - no matter how remote. "Be careful," I told myself.

––––

The Snow Lion Lodge, the best accommodations in the area, held about 30 visitors. The lodge was clean and had a large, wood-floored dining room filled with tables and cushioned chairs. There was a giant stove in the center of the room that provided precious heat during the cold evenings. The stove burned wood for fuel, which was a treat in itself. At this altitude, where no tree could grow, most people used dried yak dung for fuel, and burning yak dung gave off a lot of smoke. So if a room wasn't properly ventilated, the air quickly became unbreathable.

Aside from all of the other amenities offered at the Snow Lion, what I valued most was its large selection of tasty foods. The food at Base Camp was the best available, but the meals were set. Here, the simple act of being able to choose what I wanted to eat helped me regain both a degree of freedom and my appetite.

The rest of the team arrived in time for lunch, and as we sat at the dining room table I noticed a handwritten sign posted on the wall listing the day's food specials. That was new. Last time we were here there were no "daily specials." From where I sat I couldn't quite make out the words, so I walked over to see what specials were offered. Both my eyes and stomach where immediately riveted when I read "chicken sandwich." Really, a chicken sandwich? And it came with finger chips (aka french fries)! Oh my gosh!

For most of the trip, we had avoided any form of meat that could spoil. Eggs, spam, and mini hot dogs were the proteins of choice because they were deemed "safe" to eat. Remember, everything had to be grown locally (which wasn't much at 13,500 ft) or carried on a porter's back (unrefrigerated for days) up the mountain. Eating something like chicken would be taking a huge risk, but I was desperate for something different. So, I quietly approached Mingma and asked her about the chicken. She said it had been flown in by helicopter and kept frozen in her kitchen. She guaranteed me it was safe to eat. My team members were surprised when they heard me request a chicken sandwich for lunch, but within minutes almost everyone had changed their orders to the same. It was the best chicken sandwich I had ever eaten, and with the exception of breakfast, I ordered it for every meal.

———

At this point in the expedition, the simplest luxuries meant so much. For example, this lodge had a secret sit-down toilet. It was concealed behind a wooden utility door marked "Keep Out," and since Mingma liked our group, she gave us permission to use her secret treasure. The toilet, however, didn't flush. Using a tin can, I would scoop water from a barrel and dump it into the bowl; it was a form of manual flushing with which I was more than happy to comply. After spending five weeks squatting over a bucket, bottle, or bag, the ability to sit and relax was much appreciated.

There was also a communal sink near the lodge's entryway. It was the only one, and used for everything: washing clothes, hands and faces, and brushing teeth. There was a bucket on the shelf above the sink, and if you timed it right, you'd find warm, sometimes even hot, water in it. Of course this water wasn't purified, so you had to bring your own for brushing teeth. A simple mistake like dipping a toothbrush into unpurified water could send a person to their bunk for days, sick with vomiting and fever.

I cannot understate my appreciation of the most humble of luxuries. Having a sink was a great improvement over brushing my teeth in my tent where I would have to spit into my pee bottle. But I must admit that the toothpaste kept that bottle smelling fresh and minty. At this point, everything was relative.

The Snow Lion also proudly boasted of having the best bakery in the village. Imagine sitting at a plastic table, in a plastic chair, in a small courtyard, gazing at the snow-capped Himalayan Mountains, while eating a freshly baked cinnamon roll and drinking a cup of hot chocolate. Now that was living, and the only thing missing for me was Larry.

———

The next morning I woke up to sunlight shining through the pink curtains of my window. It was very cold, but I had slept with my extra jacket inside my sleeping bag, so it was nice and warm when I put in on. After taking my medication, I went outside to admire the view. The village was spread out further up the valley, and through its center was a single, dirt path lined with small farms, houses, inns, and an occasional shop.

My first priority was to call Larry on the satellite phone, but I had to wait until Scott or Bill came out of their room so I could borrow it. Bill came out first. One of his luxury items, although I think he would qualify it as a necessity, was a small coffee-bean grinder. After getting me the phone, Bill sat down to the task of grinding his beans. Both he and Scott loved freshly ground coffee.

As usual, I had to walk around outside trying to locate a satellite connection. First, I tried high-ground near the lodge; no connection. Next, I went across the dirt pathway toward a yak pasture; nothing. Then, I stood on the stone wall surrounding the side of the lodge; still no connection. It was cold out and my fingers were numb, but I wasn't about to give up. After roughly 15 minutes and four disconnections, while standing up the hill behind the lodge I finally got through, and it was definitely worth the effort. I talked with both Larry and Teshia, and hearing their voices warmed me from the inside out. With a smile on my face, I went into the dining room to wait for breakfast.

For breakfast that morning I had apple pancakes with two fried eggs and toast. I'd lost a lot of weight and I needed to eat as much as I could to regain some of it. After breakfast, I did my laundry. Because it was so cold, clothes had to be washed and hung out early in the day if they were to have any chance of completely drying. In fact, it usually took two days for clothes to dry. So I'd leave them outside in the sun during the day, and would bring them into my room at night, and hang them on the nails. If they didn't dry on the second day, I would sleep with the clothes in my sleeping bag and use my body heat to finish the process.

———

For the next few days I made my own schedule, which meant no schedule. There was no rush to do anything and no special time to be anywhere. I came and went as I pleased. If I missed a meal, it was no big deal. I would just walk over to the bakery and see what was coming out of the oven; whatever it was would do just fine.

———

It was now after 9:30 AM, and I knew the Internet café would be open, so I gathered up my money and glasses, and headed up the path. The Internet café was at the upper end of the village. At a relaxed pace, it usually took about 20 minutes to get there, and time was something I had plenty of. I enjoyed the leisurely walk through the village. The people were going about their daily business: herding yaks, cutting sod, washing clothes, playing cards, or just sitting around talking. We exchanged smiles as I passed. When I entered the Internet café, the young man who worked there cheerfully greeted me and showed me to his best computer. I had frequented his establishment on the way to Base Camp, and during that time, we had become friends.

That morning I posted this message on my website:

Deadly Politeness

Last night I was thinking about this entire Everest climb. So far my posts have been short and just-the-facts, but as the day approaches for us to leave for our summit attempt, things are taking on a whole different feel. We have been up the mountain twice, all gear is in place, and we are ready to go. However, this is not an endeavor to be taken lightly, and I hope I have not given that impression.

There have already been some summits and the mountain has also claimed a few souls.

I had an experience coming down the Khumbu Icefall last week that I have spent a great deal of time thinking about. It has to do with the good in human nature. When I have more time I will tell you about it.

I walked back to the lodge, checked my laundry, and placed my lunch order for a chicken sandwich. When I entered the dining room, I was happy to see that there were several groups of people inside; some were playing cards while others were just sitting around talking and sipping tea. It was an unspoken custom in the lodges that teams sat together and, if possible, left some distance between each other. It was done both as a courtesy and as a way to minimize disease transmission. Keeping with that, I sat by myself on the other side of the room, but I could hear that many of the people were speaking English, and before long, I was engaged in a conversation with three members of a trekking team. They had been at the lodge for a day or so and were leaving in the morning.

As it grew closer to lunch time, people slowly filed into the room, and soon everyone was chatting about the latest news, the weather, and where they had come from or were headed to next. During the trek to Base Camp, we kept quiet about being Everest climbers. The majority of the people we met were trekkers, and trekkers and climbers had completely different mind-sets. Trekkers were usually there to hike through the valleys, experience the culture, and admire the fantastic views. Climbers, however, were preparing for a challenge of a lifetime. By that time, we had been up the mountain twice and were feeling more confident and excited about the climb, and it wasn't long before that was revealed in the course of conversation. Turns out, there were other climbers in the room, and after a brief discussion, we wished each other good luck, and left it at that.

After lunch, I wandered off to my room. I had a book, but between my poor vision and the bad lighting, I couldn't read. So I took a nap. When I woke up, I went out to check on my laundry. It was drying, but the sun would be setting soon, so I brought the clothes into my room and hung them on the nails. I purified some water and rearranged my stuff, basically just tried to kill time.

After all, the purpose of this visit to Dingboche was to rest and recover. So far I had gotten plenty of rest and the cuts on my fingers were beginning to heal, but my cough wasn't getting any better. I'd heard that Dr. Hackett was staying in a nearby village, and I figured that at some point I should hike over and try to find him.

It started to get dark, so I grabbed my gloves, journal, water bottle, and headlamp, and headed for the dining room. Mingma fired-up the stove around 5 PM, and that brought others out of their rooms in search of heat and a card game. Vivian, Ania, and Bill appeared first. Scott showed up later toting a box of red wine. Party time! We all quickly finished the tea in our cups and passed them down to Scott. Mingma appeared soon after, and a parade of plates followed her out of the kitchen. As usual I had a chicken sandwich with finger chips, but that night I also had a cup of wine. Okay, maybe it was two.

After dinner I went to my room and snuggled into my sleeping bag. It had been a good day and I felt a sense of contentment. As a treat, I watched a movie on my iTouch. I picked *Bucket List*. I'd seen it many times and each time I was transported deeper into the story. Although it was fiction, the story was so close to my own. It's all about the importance of living life and following dreams, and making the most of the one go-around we get. The ending makes most people sad, but it makes me smile. It's a perfect ending. I hope to be so lucky.

———

I had to constantly remind myself to stay focused while in Dingboche. It was wonderful to be out of a tent and have some basic luxuries, but I hadn't come down for comfort. I had come out of necessity. I was in Nepal to climb a mountain – a mountain that had already claimed three lives this season.

———

I woke up to another bright, sunny day, but this day was special. It was May 9th, Mother's Day! I put on my jackets, hat, and gloves, and walked out into the courtyard. I stood in the crisp, fresh morning air watching a baby yak playing in the field across the way. The tiny yak ran wildly through the field weaving in and out and around the adult yaks. They paid the baby no mind, allowing it the carefree folly of youth. Finally, the tiny yak wore itself out and lay down next to its mother. I walked into the dining room with cold hands and a warm heart.

Bill was already out of his room and sitting in a chair grinding his coffee beans. As I poured myself a cup of lemon tea, we exchanged quiet good mornings. The other groups had already left on their next adventure, so Bill and I had the dining room to ourselves. I walked over to where the sun was shining through the window and sat in its warming rays. I was content, sipping my tea as I gazed out into the day.

The rest of our group showed up within the hour. We were the only guests for breakfast, but more people were due to arrive later that day. I had veggie fried noodles, two fried eggs, and toast with peanut butter. I was trying to eat as much as I could, and as often as I could, around the timing of my medications. I knew that as soon as I got back up high, my appetite would disappear and eating would once again become a battle.

I walked to the Internet café after breakfast. For the past three days, the Internet had allowed me to be with Larry and Teshia, to read about their days and tell them about mine. This connection had healed my heart and my spirit, but our temporary reunion was about to end. Tomorrow, we were leaving to hike back up to Base Camp to prepare for the summit climb, and the realization of my dream. I should be happy, excited, but I wasn't. "Everest, you bring me such a tangle of emotions!"

For hours I sat in the cold, quiet Internet café sending and reading e-mails, posting to my blog, and uploading pictures. When I finished, I said farewell to the young man who worked at the Internet café, and headed back to my room at the lodge. As I walked down the dirt path, I passed a mare nursing her foul, and thought, "how appropriate." It was Mother's Day.

———

That afternoon, Dr. Peter Hackett just happened to be walking past our lodge, and saw Scott sitting at the courtyard table. Scott and Dr. Hackett had worked together in Alaska, but they hadn't seen each other for many years. Dr. Hackett is the world's leading high-altitude medical researcher, and director of the Institute of Altitude Medicine at Telluride, Colorado. He was not only a researcher, but also a climber, and had summited Mt. Everest in 1981.

What a great coincidence. I had planned to hike over to Pheriche and seek Dr. Hackett's medical advice about my cough, but he had inadvertently come to me. Although I had never met Dr. Hackett, we had been corresponding for almost a year regarding the physiological aspects of me climbing

Everest with Wegener's Granulomatosis. I walked up and introduced myself. He immediately knew who I was. How many people with Wegener's were trying to climb Mt. Everest?

We invited him to stay for lunch and I suggested the chicken sandwich. "Chicken sandwich!?!" was his very surprised reaction. This was Dr. Hackett's umpteenth time to Nepal and he knew, all too well, the risks of eating meat. We assured him that we'd all been eating it, but he wasn't taking any chances. He respectfully asked Mingma to show him how the chicken was stored and prepared; once his inspection was completed, he ordered it for lunch. Before we had a chance to finish our sandwiches, Mingma delivered a plate of freshly baked cinnamon rolls to our table. Dr. Hackett, like all of us, couldn't resist these wonderful treats, and he stayed for a while.

During the course of the meal, I asked Dr. Hackett about my cough. After discussing the details, he suggested that I stop by the Everest ER when I got back to Base Camp. He called it "The Khumbu Cough," and assured my climbing group that it wasn't contagious. They were all very relieved, but I was left thinking, "Nice, I have a cough named after the deadly icefall!"

Dr. Hackett was still visiting with everyone late that afternoon when I stood up to leave the courtyard. As a Mother's Day gift to myself, I was going to take a hot shower, and Mingma's shower was one of the best I'd seen. It was a closet-sized shed with a two-by-three foot enclosed porch. The porch had a chair on which to sit, and there were nails on the wall to hang clothes and a towel (if you had one). The only uncomfortable thing about the shower was the icy wind that worked its way into the tiny shed from several different directions. With that in mind, I scheduled my shower for 3 PM, hoping the wind wouldn't be too cold, but it was.

———

I woke up the next morning and packed my gear. After breakfast, we donned our packs and got ready to leave. We were hiking back to Base Camp, and then making a try for the summit. I should have been excited, but instead I felt sad. This would be the last time I would see Mingma. After our summit attempt, we would take a different route out of the valley and wouldn't be passing through Dingboche, so this was goodbye. Before we left, Mingma draped a silk blessing scarf (called a khata) around our necks and gave each of us a big hug. She stood in the courtyard of the Snow Lion Lodge, waving and wishing us luck as we walked away.

———

We hiked up to Loboche (15,000 ft) and spent the night. By late morning on May 11th we were back at Base Camp, where we were scheduled to rest a few days before leaving for our summit attempt. What we didn't know at the time, was that there might not be another summit-window this season.

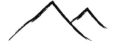

Chapter 11

TO SUMMIT OR NOT TO SUMMIT?

After months of preparation, everything was finally ready. The mountain was roped to the summit, the higher camps were staked out, all our supplies were in place, and the team was rested and ready to go.

On May 12th, we were back at Base Camp and scheduled to leave for our summit attempt in the morning. To go for the summit, we needed a five to six day window of acceptable weather, but the weather had changed for the worse. The Jet Stream returned over Everest and 70-80 MPH winds ravaged the upper mountain. The projected weather-window had now shortened to what appeared to be two "okay" days for the actual summit climb *if* we were already staged at a higher camp. The stronger winds and colder temperatures made it more dangerous to go for the summit. Climbing teams on both the south and north sides of the mountain were struggling with the same decision: go tomorrow and hope for success or wait at Base Camp and hope for a better opportunity.

The "not knowing" made it a very difficult day. We had to wait for the latest weather forecast to come in sometime after lunch, but we also had to be ready just in case the decision was made to go. So, we spent the day packing our gear and getting our affairs in order. The waiting was nerve-racking.

This was the culmination of everything I had been working toward for the past three years. If I didn't make it, for whatever reason, I wouldn't be back. This was my one chance to summit Everest.

Scott and Bill called us into the dining tent about 3 PM. They explained the details of the situation and then put the question before the team: did we want to go tomorrow and try for the summit knowing the risks or were we willing to wait for the next window, which was predicted to open in five days? It was a huge decision. If we passed up the shorter, more dangerous attempt, we would be placing our only hope of summiting Everest on a window that might not actually appear. The verdict was unanimous; none of us were willing to risk our lives to summit a mountain. For us, this window was closed.

———

For days, strong winds battered the upper camps. There were reports of frostbite and tents being destroyed. The climbers who had decided to go up were fighting for their chance to summit. If they survived the conditions at the upper camps, they might be rewarded with a two-day window when the winds were predicted to drop, and they could attempt to summit.

During this time, everything on the mountain was directed by the weather. The climbers going for summit were staged at Camp 3, and waiting for the weather-window to open. More than a mile below, not even Base Camp escaped the ravages of the high winds, but at least we were safe. As we waited, my thoughts kept drifting to the hardships and dangers the climbers who had gone up were experiencing. I had to continually remind myself that every person who steps foot on Everest accepts the consequences that come with that decision.

———

Predicting the weather on Everest was nearly impossible. Even using the most modern, computerized forecast reports, Scott and Bill could only get a rough idea of the weather for a 10-day period. They spent hour after hour, day after day, studying those forecasts in an attempt to predict when the next window might open. I didn't presume (and still don't) to understand the complexities of those high-tech forecasts, but from what I was told, they're somewhat contradictory and unreliable. They were, however, the best information available. Realistically, Scott and Bill could only predict about five days ahead, and at that point, it wasn't looking good. They saw a possible window opening around May 22nd, but a cyclone was moving our way from the Bay of Bengal.

The days ticked by as we waited at Base Camp. If this window didn't materialize, there would be no summit for us this year. It was nearing the end of May, and the end of the climbing season. Very soon, the Khumbu Icefall would become too unstable, and the Icefall Doctors would remove the ladders, closing the south side of Everest. Time was running out.

———

Aside from the weather, I was very concerned that something else might stop me from making the summit – my terrible cough! I needed to go see a doctor. I walked through camp searching for the Everest ER clinic. We had walked past the clinic on our way into Base Camp, but that was a month ago, and now I was having trouble locating it in the ever-changing maze of tents and twisting ice. As I meandered through camp, I heard my name. At first I thought I was hearing things, but then I heard it again. I looked around and saw Dawa, our head Sherpa, standing on the hillside. He was visiting a friend and saw me wandering about. I asked him where the medical clinic was and he pointed me in the correct direction.

The clinic was a large, white tent nestled into a gully, which was why it was so hard for me to find. I heard voices coming from inside as I approached, but I didn't want to just walk in, so I called out. A young man appeared, and I asked to see Dr. Hackett. He told me to wait. A few minutes later, Dr. Hackett emerged from a large, orange tent higher up on the hill. As it turned out, that was the medical staff's dining tent. I hoped I hadn't interrupted his meal. Dr. Hackett greeted me, and we walked into the white medical tent. Inside, there was another doctor helping a local man. As I looked around I was surprised by the clinic's seemingly limited resources, but Dr. Hackett assured me that they could work wonders within those white walls. And I believed him.

After the local man left, Dr. Hackett introduced me to Dr. Steve Halvorson. I liked him immediately. Dr. Steve, as he liked to be called, wore a big smile on his face and a baseball cap decorated with a large, white artificial flower. We exchanged greetings as he directed me to sit down on one of the cots. Dr. Hackett sat at the small table next to me and asked me to describe my condition. I told him that I'd had the cough for almost four weeks, had already tried a round of antibiotic medication, and had spent four days at a lower altitude, but nothing had helped. And with our summit attempt coming up (I hoped), I was extremely worried about my condition. Dr. Hackett conducted a brief exam confirmed that I had "The Khumbu Cough," and suggested that I try an inhaler. He said, with a little luck, the cough would be almost gone by the time we went for the summit. Feeling relieved, I paid for the inhaler and thanked both of the doctors.

———

The Everest ER is a nonprofit medical clinic at Base Camp. Founded in 2003 by Dr. Luanne Freer, this high-altitude clinic provides valuable medical services. For the 2010 climbing season it was staffed by an amazing group of volunteer doctors:

Dr. Luanne Freer (founder and director of the Everest ER), Dr. Peter Hackett (director of the Institute for Altitude Medicine and Everest summiter in 1981), and Dr. Steve Halvorson (emergency doctor and instructor for the Wilderness Medical Association). Lakpa Norbu Sherpa served as the clinic's logistics manager. This temporary clinic provided services to anyone in need of medical care: climbers, Sherpas, porters, trekkers, and even a dog that had wandered in with a broken leg. According to the patient log, between April 4th and May 27th, 2010, the clinic had 445 patient visits, several of which had been made by me.

———

After returning from the Everest ER, I decided to sit in the dining tent instead of my own, just for a change. As I sat mindlessly staring out the doorway, I was roused from my languorous state by a large group of Sherpas walking by. Strange. I got up, walked outside, and watched as about 10 Sherpas walked past the tent and into Base Camp, two of whom were carrying something. That wasn't unusual since the main route to the Khumbu Icefall was from this side of Base Camp, and people were always going by transporting equipment and supplies. What was unusual was "what" the two Sherpas were carrying. It was a stretcher holding a body! And as the day progressed, more bodies followed.

There are many bodies locked within the Khumbu's grasp, frozen in time but not in place. The icefall is always moving, flowing down the mountain at about a rate of three feet a day. And as the season warms and the ice melts, the Khumbu opens its icy hands and releases some of those who have been held within. One of the bodies recovered was that of Ang Phinjo Sherpa, who had been killed in 2006 when a serac collapsed. His family was contacted and they came to the mountain and conducted a traditional burial ceremony for him. A total of four bodies were retrieved during our stay.

———

Days passed as we waited, and with each passing day, our bodies lost both strength and acclimatization. Humans are not designed to stay at extreme altitude for long periods, and we were living at 17,600 feet. At that altitude, the body cannot sustain itself, let alone retain the strength and acclimatization needed to climb to 29,000 feet. Our bodies were literally deteriorating as we waited for our window. We had to do something, but we couldn't go up Everest, so we decided to hike to Camp 1 on nearby Mt. Pumori (19,000 ft). This was nothing compared to what we had been doing, but it was better than sitting in our tents wasting away.

———

We headed for Mt. Pumori after breakfast. By now, we were all familiar with some of the trails on the lesser mountains across the valley from Base Camp. I started up Pumori in the same direction as Scott, Vivian, and Bill. It was a steeper section and the route looked like it would be a good workout. After a while the trail disappeared into a section of large, jagged boulders. Up until that point, I'd been moving at a good pace, but once I started jumping across the boulders, I had to slow down. It was on this type of terrain that my distorted vision became a big problem, and one poorly judged jump could end with a broken leg. After everything I'd been through to get this far, I wasn't willing to risk injuring myself on a half-day training hike.

As I came up from the right, I noticed a large group weaving its way up from the left. The trail narrowed as I neared Pumori's Camp 1, and I merged into the group. Once at the small camp, I turned around to look at Everest. From 19,000 feet, it was a stunning view of the mighty giant with its familiar white, summit plume streaking across the bright blue sky.

There were about 30 climbers sitting around chatting, snacking, and taking pictures. We were all there for the same reason: to stay trained and acclimatized. As I took off my pack I saw Russell Brice sitting on a nearby rock. The group turned out to be Russell's summit team. I'd never met Russell in person, only through e-mail. I walked over and introduced myself; he remembered me. The meeting gave me the opportunity to thank Russell in person for understanding why I had switched summit teams.

I returned from Pumori just in time for lunch. It had been great to get out of my tent and get some exercise, but as I walked into our camp, it was like stepping into a cryptic aura of apprehension. Clearly, the waiting had taken its toll on me, not just physically but mentally as well. I sat in the dining tent feeling the size of my arms and legs, and was shocked by how small they'd become; it seemed as if they were half their original size. I sat there wondering if I would even have enough physical strength left to summit. I had felt strong as a yak when I left home 44 days previously, but now, as my muscles dwindled away, I felt doubt creeping in. Time was playing a mean trick on me.

I awoke to another day of waiting and wondering. Even though there were hundreds of people at Base Camp, it was very quiet. All of the climbers who didn't go for the earlier summit window were in the same situation as me and my team. And because most of the larger teams were the ones waiting, if or when a summit-window opened, there would be a huge traffic jam on the mountain – and we all knew it!

It was just after breakfast on May 15th on Everest, but back home it was the evening of May 14th, and the night of the

CSUF faculty/staff year-end party at Dr. Beam's house. Larry had e-mailed a few days before to say that he'd be going and that it might be nice if I called. So, I picked up the satellite phone and dialed the number. Amazingly, I got right through. I heard Dr. Beam's voice say, "Hello," and the background was filled with the voices of my friends. I hesitated; it felt odd. I was standing on a glacier at the base of Mt. Everest, and they were standing in Dr. Beam's house, half a world away. To me it seemed as if they were on a different plane of existence, another world. Finally I said, "Hello, this is Cindy." There was a slight pause and then I heard Dr. Beam yell out, "Hey everyone, it's Cindy calling from Base Camp!" Dr. Beam must have held up his phone because all I could hear was a chorus of cheering voices. I talked with Dr. Beam for a few minutes, though I think I did more coughing than talking. Then there was another pause, and I heard Larry say, "Hi there."

The contact and reconnection with "home" was just what I needed. I put the sat phone back in the dining tent and walked outside feeling revitalized. The weather was actually pleasant (meaning the sun was shining and the temperature was above freezing), and while it wasn't my day for a bath, I felt like washing my hair. So I went back to my tent, grabbed my tiny blue towel, and headed for the river. Standing on a large, flat rock suspended over the cold rushing water, I poured shampoo in my hands and started scrubbing. By the time I was done, my hands and scalp were numb. The river water was actually glacial melt and only a few degrees above freezing, but a few minutes of unpleasantness was worth having kind-of clean hair. After more than six weeks of "unpleasantness," I had developed a new perspective of its meaning, and a few minutes of freezing cold hands and scalp just didn't qualify.

Now that I was more presentable (which meant I could appear in public without wearing my hat), I walked to the medical clinic to see Dr. Hackett about my cough. He advised me to continue using the inhaler, and Dr. Steve agreed. At this point, it was all that could be done. Before I left the clinic, I invited both doctors to our camp for dinner. I didn't know who did their cooking, but I knew we had the best cook on the mountain and told them so. They accepted with an enthusiastic, "See you at six."

————

I spent the rest of the day in my tent playing what I lovingly refer to as "The Tent Game." We were in high-altitude mountaineering tents, and to the smallest detail, they were designed so that nothing could get in, thus protecting the occupant(s) against the harsh Alpine environment. When properly secured they could withstand 100 MPH winds, snow blizzards, and rain storms. There was, however, a trade-off: more protection meant less tent-breathability (air flow). So the game was based on internal tent temperature, also known as, "To unzip or not to unzip: that is the question."

When the sun was out, the inside of the tent would get hot, unbearably hot. At times it was like being in an oddly-shaped, orange sauna. In order to cool the tent, I would unzip its doors and vents, but then the clouds would move in, blocking the sun, and cause the temperature to plummet. So, I would have to zip everything up again. After the clouds passed, the temperature would instantly climb back to boiling, so down would go the zippers. Up and down, up and down, until I'd succumb to laziness and let the tent win the game.

————

It was now May 16th and the ambiguous weather forecasts were going to force our hand, but what cards would we play? We had to contend with the movement of the Jet Stream, the cyclone headed our direction, and the fact that we were running out of time. A decision had to be made, and soon. In the meantime, we just sat around doing a lot of nothing. The waiting and not knowing were agonizing, a spiritual and emotional demon from which the only escape was to pack up and go home, and that wasn't happening, at least not with me! But I had to do something. I had to get out of camp, and there was only one logical place to go – back up Mt. Pumori. As I hiked, a single thought kept replaying in my head, "Maybe there wasn't going to be another summit-window." Step after step, hour after hour, it kept at me. I tried, but I couldn't shut it off! That demon just kept haunting me!

I actually felt the hope slipping away for the first time, seeping slowly through my fingers and out of my grasp. After all the years and all my struggles, I might not get *my* chance. As I hiked down Pumori and headed back to Base Camp, I became increasingly saddened by the reality of the situation. I had always known that it was a possibility, and months ago I had told myself that if I wasn't allowed to summit Everest, for whatever reason, it would be "okay." But as the days turned into hours and the hours ticked down to minutes, I realized it did matter – a lot!

———

I never felt as alive as I did while climbing Mt. Everest. It took me to the highest high, but the waiting, wondering, and loneliness took me to the lowest low. Each day, each hour of waiting and hoping, became an ever-increasing struggle, a battle between my psyche and my soul. "I am strong!" I told myself, "I know I can do this, if Everest will let me!"

———

Today was Ania's birthday. After dinner Scott dimmed the lights in the dining tent and Serki entered carrying a beautifully decorated cake. Its white frosting was alight with candles, and multicolored candies encircled the edges. Amazing! Suddenly the tent filled with Sherpas and we all sang happy birthday. Somehow Ania managed to gather enough air in her lungs to blow out the candles, but to her surprise – they didn't go out. They were trick candles! We all started laughing; this was just what we needed. When the candles were finally extinguished, colorfully wrapped gifts appeared on the table in front of Ania (I have no idea how they procured them). Wearing her new pink scarf, Ania started dancing inside the tent and we all joined in. After circling the table in the dining tent a few times, Ania lead the conga line of dancers into the kitchen tent to the surprise of the dining Sherpas! Wide-eyed and smiling, they cheered and clapped as we went prancing and dancing through their tent and then disappeared into the darkness. After so much calm reserve, it was great to let loose and have some much-needed carefree fun. When the party was over, I walked back to my tent with a smile on my face.

Ania's Birthday Party. (Photo courtesy of Ania Lichota)

On May 17th after the weather reports came in, the decision was made: we would leave for our summit attempt early the next morning!!!! We might not make it all the way, but we were going to try!

My cough still hadn't cleared up, so I went to see Dr. Hackett one last time. The only thing he could do was to prescribe me another inhaler, which did seem to be of some help. Before leaving the tent, I stopped and looked into Dr. Hackett's eyes, and told him how much it meant to me to know that if something happened to me while I was high on the mountain, he was at Base Camp. Dr. Hackett was the only person who had any idea of the complications I might experience because of my medical condition. I can't explain "why" the idea of his presence, so many thousands of feet below, mattered. Logically, it didn't make sense. It wasn't as if he could come up or I could easily get down if something went wrong, but somehow knowing he was there gave me comfort.

The last journal entry I wrote the evening before leaving Base Camp for our summit attempt:

We are going for the summit tomorrow (leaving at 3 AM)! Larry and Teshia I love you and promise to come down safe!

Chapter 12

THE WINDOW IS CLOSING

The last blog post I wrote the day before leaving Base Camp for our summit attempt:

Leaving for the Summit

We are leaving for our summit bid tomorrow! It will take us about five days up and two days to get down. I will be able to post from Camp 2 and will TRY to make a call from the summit. This is it: the culmination off all the years of training, preparation, and leaving my family for what seems to be forever. Mother Nature, however, is always in charge and safety is first. With that in mind – we are off!

———

My last thought before closing my eyes the night before leaving for the summit: "I left home 48 days ago to climb the World's highest mountain. During that time I have experienced both the anticipated and the unimaginable of physical and psychological extremes. Tomorrow I leave for the final, most challenging part of this journey, and whatever is to come, I feel confident that I will make the right decisions."

———

At 3 AM on May 18th, I circled the Puja chorten three times
and headed into the darkness toward the Khumbu Icefall. It
had been 12 days since we had last climbed through the icefall, and it had changed. I looked up into the cloudless night
thinking, "This is it, my one chance to summit Mt. Everest."
As I made my way up the lower part of the icefall, I could see
dozens of headlamps ahead of me, and just as many behind.
Like us, all of the waiting climbers were now on their way up
the mountain. I was glad we got an early start, and hoped we
wouldn't get stuck in too many traffic jams; the Khumbu Icefall is no place to stand around waiting!

———

To my surprise, we only experienced a few minor delays
going up, mostly waiting to cross ladders, and the entire team
reached the top of the icefall in about four hours. As I traversed the vast crevasse-filled section between the icefall and
Camp 1, I was amazed at how much of the glacier had disappeared! What used to be small crevasses had become huge valleys; the glacier was melting! I wondered what it would be like
on our way down.

We stopped at Camp 1 for a short break before heading
across the Western Cwm and on to Camp 2. I ate a package of
trail mix, drank some water, and adjusted my clothes. It was
a sunny, windless day, and even though it was only 8 AM, the
temperature was already rising. The last time I crossed the
Cwm it was unbearably hot, and I feared this day would be
worse. The trick was to remove enough layers to protect me
from the elements while still allowing me to stay cool.

This was our third trip up the mountain and we were
familiar with the route. As usual, we started off as a group but
quickly spread out. After a while I came to the most unstable
ladder in Western Cwm. I'd crossed the other ladders without
the aid of another climber holding the side ropes, but this dou-

ble ladder was too dangerous and I wasn't going to risk trying it alone, so I waited for a group coming up from behind. On the mountain, it didn't matter what language you spoke, everyone understood what was needed or being asked. As the group neared, I asked the lead person to hold the rope; this was an accepted, almost expected, practice. As the climber reached down and held up the two ropes, I noticed that both were out of alignment with the ladder. One extended too far off to one side, and the other was too short. In an effort to make crossing safer, someone had added a third rope about halfway across the ladder. It certainly wasn't ideal, but that was the way of it, and I started across. When I was about half way across the ladder, the person holding the rope lost his grip, and the rope snapped. I heard the gasps from the climbers behind me as I struggled to regain my balance. I managed to stay on the ladder, but my pole was ripped off my wrist and went plummeting into the crevasse below. My orange trekking pole with "Cindy" written on it became part of Mt. Everest. Maybe one day it will make its way down the icefall and someone will find it and wonder about "Cindy." I'm just glad it was my pole, and not me, that remained on Everest.

———

A little while later, I noticed that I was slowing down. Granted, I was tired from climbing the icefall and it was a very hot day, not to mention that I was also at an altitude of over 21,000 feet, but I felt unusually weak and nauseous. Vivian came up from behind and asked how I was doing. I told him that I was fine; I just had no energy. He suggested that I do what he was doing: count steps. Go to 100 and start over; it distracts the mind and keeps the body moving. So I tried it. For the first hour or so I counted to 100, but I started having difficulty remembering the numbers so I switched to counting to 50. I was still having trouble concentrating and the nausea was getting worse, so I finally gave up counting altogether. I needed a break.

The Western Cwm was full of hidden crevasses and snow bridges, making it very unsafe to wander far from the trail, so I stepped a few feet off to the side, sat down, and took off my pack. I tried to eat some crackers, but almost threw-up. The only thing I could keep down was a little water. After resting for several minutes, I got up and continued toward Camp 2. On the scale of climbing Everest, the distance wasn't that far. At my normal pace, I would have already been at Camp 2, but I was moving ever slower, and I'd only get about 300 yards before needing to sit down again.

As I sat there, Ania walked up to me and asked if I was okay. I said, "Yes, I'm just very weak today." She told me that I didn't look good, that I was pale, but I insisted that I was fine and would be right behind her. Thank goodness she didn't listen to me. Ania turned to her Sherpa and asked him to call Scott on the radio. I tried to stop him, but Ania was insistent. Scott answered the radio and the Sherpa handed it to me. Scott asked, "What's up?" I said, "I'm fine, just nauseous and going very slowly." Ania interrupted, and told me to tell Scott that I looked "like shit," and to send a Sherpa down to take my pack. So I said those exact words to Scott followed by, "I'm fine, just weak." And *those words* were barely out of my mouth when I started falling over; I was losing consciousness. Ania said, "Cindy, you are passing out! Tell Scott to send a Sherpa down!" So again I repeated Ania's words into the radio, and Scott sent the Sherpa.

I got to Camp 2 at noon. It had taken me four hours to cross the Western Cwm. After thanking the Sherpa and retrieving my pack, I walked over and sat on a rock outside of my tent. That was disappointing and scary! If I couldn't make it across the Western Cwm, how was I going to summit Everest? Within minutes I began feeling physically better and I thought, "WOW, what was that?" As it turned out, I had suffered a bout of heat exhaustion. For a while I couldn't believe it because I'd never actually felt hot! Then I remembered my first aid training: hello – not feeling hot was one of the symptoms!

———

To make matters worse, as soon as I got to Camp 2, I completely lost my appetite. I sat at the table in the dining tent trying to avoid my lunch. I couldn't look at it, smell it, much less eat it, but I knew that I had to. After about five minutes, I worked up the courage to take a bite. I didn't know what I was eating, nor did I care, but I forced that food into my mouth. Tears ran down my face as I tried to swallow. I finally gave up and went to my tent. It had not been a good day.

———

I woke up the next morning feeling better about everything. At breakfast, I managed to eat a half of a bowl of porridge and drink a cup of instant hot chocolate. It was a scheduled rest day, and weather permitting, we would move up to Camp 3 the following day. Because we had to wait at Base Camp seven days longer than planned, it was especially important to regain some of our acclimatization before attempting even higher elevations.

It was cold and snowing outside, so I spent most of the day in my tent. As I snuggled in my sleeping bag, I reflected back on the experience as a whole. Prior to this I had only looked ahead, planning for the next task, but in retrospect, it had been a very successful expedition. Sure, we had our bouts of minor illnesses, and experienced a few bumps and weather curveballs, but considering the extreme environment, everything to this point had gone quite well. We were leaving for Camp 3 the next day, on our way to the top of the world! It was quite exciting, only excitement at 21, 600 feet was experienced in a much more subdued fashion.

Later that afternoon we got a satellite connection and I made this blog post:

Going for the Mt. Everest Summit

We are at Camp 2 (21,600 ft). I suffered a minor bout of heat exhaustion from crossing the Western Cwm. I will send pictures tomorrow. We leave for Camp 3 in the morning, Camp 4 the following day, and then the summit. There are many variables which may affect our progress: weather being a big question, and because many climbers have been waiting for the weather, there could be big crowds on the mountain. If we get slowed by either weather or the 150 climbers on the fixed lines, we may have to turn around because we will not have enough oxygen. Whatever happens, we will give it our best shot, but Mother Nature (and maybe my medical condition) will decide. Our team and Sherpas are in place and we leave in the morning. I will not be able to post. However, my blog manager may be able to post media updates. Also, watch the Mountain Trip site.

I want to thank you all for your support. Knowing you are there is amazing! Leaving my family for months, managing my medical condition, and climbing Mt. Everest is unimaginably difficult, but here I am!

I, however, have every intention of standing on the top of the world holding the NORD Banner!!!!!!!!

To all of you who think you cannot follow your dreams, please try! You never know what is possible until you try. Remember, when life brings us a storm: we must learn to dance in the rain.

Please excuse my writing, lack of oxygen!

The satellite phone would be our only form of communication with the outside world the moment we left Camp 2 in our bid for the summit. Consequently, as we waited at Camp 2, everyone tried to post as much information as possible before we "disappeared" into thin air.

———

At 5 AM on May 20th, we headed for the Lhotse Face and Camp 3. It was a bright, sunny day and the winds had died down. It usually took about 45 minutes to walk up the gradually sloping section from Camp 2 to the base of the Lhotse Face, but looking up, I saw that there was already a long line of climbers on the rope going to Camp 3. All season long, this was exactly what every climber tried to avoid – traffic jams on the mountain. This season, like many in the past, the weather had forced the climbers into the same window-of-opportunity. Give or take a day, anyone who wanted to summit had to go up or go home.

———

As we approached the base, the winds once again picked up. Within minutes the Lhotse Face was assaulted by winds strong enough to send snow swirling all the way across its icy slopes, battering climbers and tents with its destructive force. Scott stopped and looked up the mountain. Due to a lifetime of Alpine experience, he had developed an uncanny ability to analyze the conditions and assess the situation. As we stood watching and waiting, Scott considered the multitude of variables involved in making the potentially life-threatening decision to continue up the mountain. Finally, Scott turned and said that these were the strongest winds he'd ever seen on this part of the mountain. That was quite a powerful statement coming from him: a four-time Everest summiter. There wasn't a hint of disagreement when Scott announced that we were aborting the climb and returning to Camp 2.

———

Safety, not the summit, was my number one priority, and I had signed on with Mountain Trip and Scott because that was their focus as well. Both Bill and Scott were extremely experienced high-altitude guides. And in case we were delayed at any of the high Camps, they had arranged for extra supplies and oxygen, along with plenty of Sherpa-support. Those were the kinds of things that added an extra margin of safety, and to me, they were worth every penny of the higher financial cost of climbing Everest.

Like any sport, there are different types of climbers, and each one tackles Everest with their individual skill set, philosophy, and goals. For example, very experienced high-altitude climbers feel comfortable handling all aspects of the climb themselves (i.e., supplies, food, equipment, logistics, etc.), and some even prefer to climb solo. Others may use basic Base Camp support services and access to weather reports, and climb with a Sherpa only, no guide. And then there are climbers like me, who choose what's referred to as "full-support service," where all of those things are managed by a company or individual.

Everyone who sets foot on Everest decides what they want from the experience, and accepts the risks associated with those choices. My view is, "To each their own," and I knew my level of experience and never pretended to be more than I was. Sure, I could clip on and follow a rope up the mountain, but I had very little experience predicting weather, and I had never climbed using bottled oxygen. For me, the only responsible way to climb Mt. Everest was with the support of a professional guiding company.

———

We got back down to Camp 2 just in time to watch the Jet Stream move back over Everest. I stood outside my tent looking up, transfixed by the growing chaos. The Lhotse Face was being battered by winds spiraling in from every direction, winds that were constantly changing right before my eyes! And above, the brilliant blue sky provided the perfect backdrop to watch the Jet Stream as it spun clouds into all types of crazy patterns! As I stood there, a feeling of dread began creeping into my thoughts, "What would happen to the climbers already up there, and would this be as far as we were going to get?"

The Jet Stream returns over the Lhotse Face and Everest. (Photo from Camp 2)

My last blog post from Camp 2:

Jet Stream Over Mt. Everest – Not Good!

Today we tried to climb the Lhotse Face and get to Camp 3, but we were turned back by high winds. Later in the morning the Jet Stream came in over Mt. Everest (100 MPH winds). We lay in our tents listening to the roar of the wind moving over the summit. The site is beautiful but not when you are counting the DAYS left to summit this season! Imagine being here for over 7 weeks: waiting and trying and hoping.

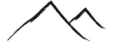

Chapter 13

AFTER FIFTY-ONE DAYS

The winds had died down during the night and we awoke to a calm, clear morning, just the day we'd been waiting for! Fantastic! It looked like we were going to get our chance to go for the summit after all or at least to get to Camp 3. We put on our gear and, once again, headed for the Lhotse Face. I looked up the mountain as we approached, and for as far as I could see, a line of tiny black dots was slowly moving up the fixed rope. I turned and glanced behind me and saw an even longer line of climbers. Everyone was on the move. Once we reached the base of the Lhotse Face, we quickly clipped on and began our ascent. The first section was a bit challenging, but once I cleared it, the terrain transformed into a vast field of steep, blue ice.

———

It was now around midday and while I couldn't see it, I knew I had to be getting close to our camp. I'd already passed some tents staked-out on the lower, flatter section, but our camp was higher up, and higher up was better. We would be climbing into what's known as the "Death Zone" the next day, so we wanted to be as high up as possible to start. As I clipped past a resting climber, I looked up and saw that the next section was very steep, maybe 60 or 70 degrees. I was tired, and it felt like someone had stolen all of the oxygen from the air. At almost 23,500 feet, each breath only contained about 42% of the oxygen compared to sea level. With so little oxygen, I had to take three or four breaths for every step I took. I lowered my head and went to back to work, climbing in a kind of hypnotic haze.

After a while, I looked up and saw that I was approaching what appeared to be a large crevasse off to my right. As I neared the crack, I realized that it was actually a small shelf, and that there were tents on it - our tents! I had finally reached Camp 3! Smiling, I hung on the rope and examined the ledge. It was very narrow, just wide enough for one tent and nothing more. I unclipped from the main fixed line and carefully made my way over to the ledge. The ledge (or shelf) was a natural formation where part of the ice face had collapsed inward, creating a fairly flat 20-by-60 foot area between an ice wall and a 3,000 foot, sheer drop-off. With just a foot or so between the tents and the edge, one misstep or slip would send me tumbling thousands of feet down the Lhotse Face. In our hypoxic state, it was best not to walk around. So once everyone arrived, we settled into our tents and didn't come out again until it was time to leave the next morning.

Happy to be at Camp 3 (near 24,000 ft).
(Photo by Vivian Rigney)

Camp 3 on the Lhotse Face with Mt. Everest in the background.

At almost 24,000 feet, I would sleep using oxygen for the first time. We had an early start in the morning, and I was going to try and get to sleep as soon as possible. I secured my tent and gear, ate some cheese and crackers, drank a cup of instant soup, took the rest of my pills, and wearing my big down suit, wriggled into my sleeping bag. I grabbed my oxygen mask, adjusted the straps, and then checked the hose and regulator connections. Satisfied, I set the bottle in front of me and opened the valve to 0.5 liters per minute (the standard oxygen flow rate for low-level activity and sleeping). Then I wedged the oxygen bottle between my sleeping bag and my pack, and lay down. I felt the effects of the oxygen almost instantly. My breathing slowed and my muscles relaxed as an aura of calm came over me.

My alarm went off at 3 AM. I had two hours before we were scheduled to leave, but getting ready takes a long time at extreme altitude. My first night sleeping on oxygen wasn't bad. I had slept quite well, and I was sure my teammates had too, since my oxygen mask muffled my continuous coughing. In fact, the big, yellow mask covered my face, keeping it warm during the freezing-cold night, and the hose and bottle weren't a problem either, just more gear to manage. The benefits of having the supplemental oxygen far outweigh the encumbrance. It was a good start to what was supposed to be a challenging day of climbing.

I felt strong in both body and spirit, and I was pleasantly surprised that I hadn't noticed any vision problems. At extreme altitudes, many climbers experience asymptomatic high-altitude retinal hemorrhages HARH (bleeding of the blood vessels in the eye). I knew that I was at a higher risk of HARH because Wegener's damages the blood vessels. It had been less than three years since I'd had the center retinal vascular occlusion that had left me functionally blind in my left eye. Now I was at 24,000 feet and going higher, thus increasing the potential of other vascular events. I was aware of the risks and chose to continue up the mountain.

———

At this point in the climb I carried only what I needed to survive, and most of that had spent the night inside my sleeping bag, making for some uncomfortable bed partners. Comfort, however, was a thing I'd forfeited long ago. The temperature inside my tent was well below freezing and I didn't want to leave the relative warmth of my sleeping bag, but I had to get ready. I retrieved my medications and water bottle from the jumble of items inside my bag, and took my pills. Still wrapped in my sleeping bag, I slowly began to pack my backpack. Then I thought, "Wait! What about the oxygen bottle?" It had to go in along with my sleeping bag. This wasn't rocket science! I had done it hundreds of times, the sleeping bag goes in first.

Clearly, I was experiencing altitude-induced, muddle-brain. I removed everything from my pack, begrudgingly crawled out of the cozy bag, and started over. As I was re-packing, I heard Bill yell from his tent something about a hot drink. I yelled back, "No thanks, I have my own breakfast." Melting water at that altitude took a lot of time and fuel, and frankly, my cup was already packed, and I didn't want to dig it out. A cold breakfast was fine with me. I fumbled through my stuff until I found the zip-lock bag containing my food-cache. I grabbed another package of cheese and crackers, and thought, "perfect."

After I finished packing, I scooted down to the door of my tent so I could put on my boots. I had peeked out earlier to check the weather, but it had been too dark to see anything. Now the sun was up, and the sky was clear and the winds were calm, another beautiful morning. So far our weather-window was holding, but there was constant concern about the hovering Jet Stream and the approaching cyclone. The schedule was to get to Camp 4, and then see how things looked. We literally had to take it day-by-day, even hour-by-hour. On Everest, conditions could go from great to grave within a matter of minutes.

————

I felt a little dizzy when I stood up to put on my harness, but that was to be expected in this thin air. And it was only going to get worse as we continued up the mountain, which is why we'd be climbing with supplemental oxygen. Sleeping with the oxygen equipment was no big deal, but climbing wearing a mask connected to a hose, connected to a large tank inside my backpack, was going to be a new experience, but I was looking forward to the extra boost the oxygen would provide.

After donning all of my gear, I looked and felt like I was about the leave the Earth's surface and head into outer space, and in a way, I was. My morning attire consisted of several layers of clothes under a big, yellow down suit (which was akin to wearing a custom-fit sleeping bag). I wore lightweight, yellow, Frankenstein-like boots on my feet with 12-point steel crampons attached to the soles. I had a climbing harness with all manner of clips, leashes, and other equipment around my waist, and a pair of thick, black double-gloves on my hands. A lightweight, grey helmet protected my head, and amber-colored, glacier glasses shielded my eyes. Once everything was in place, I added the final accoutrements to the ensemble: a backpack containing my sleeping bag and pad, oxygen bottle, water, food, medication and extra gear, and the large, yellow oxygen mask which covered half of my face. Yup, I was now ready for take-off.

———

Using the smaller rope from Camp 3, I carefully walked over to the main fixed line and clipped on. As I stood there giving my gear a quick double-check, I looked up the steep 60 to 70 degree, windswept ice that was the final section of the Lhotse Face, and like the day before, there was no shortage of company on the rope. For as far as I could see in both directions, climbers were making their way up the single, fixed rope that we all relied upon on this especially dangerous section of steep, blue ice. Although I couldn't see exactly what was ahead, I always knew when I was approaching a difficult bit because the pace on the rope would slow to a crawl, even stop. It wasn't possible to pass anyone on this part of the Lhotse Face, so I pulled my patience out of my pocket, and waited my turn.

I'd been standing in one place for several minutes when I looked up and saw the sun's rays shining down like arms, momentarily embracing the climbers before dancing off the ice in a brilliant display of the mountain's deadly beauty. It was an incredible sight, and since I wasn't going anywhere, I pulled out my camera to take some pictures. But after one click of the shutter, my camera died. Even though I had kept it inside my down suit and next to my body, the outside air was so cold that it quickly drained my battery. I may have only gotten one shot, but it was a good one!

A beautiful morning to climb the Lhotse Face.

———

After clearing a particularly large ice-bulge, I found myself climbing up a more gradual, snow slope. Some distance ahead, I could see that the line of climbers had veered off to the left. They were leaving the Lhotse Face and heading toward a section of rock known as the Yellow Band. Until that point, my view of the route had been obscured by the steep ice wall, but once up it, I could see forever. Above me was the summit of Mt. Lhotse (not going there), below me was a line of at least 50 climbers (glad we started early), and off to my left was the fixed line with about 30 climbers on it. Then I realized that I was higher than I'd ever been before, and each step up would take me to a new personal height record! Even as I stood there, I found it hard to believe that I'd made it up the Lhotse Face and was now approaching the Yellow Band!

———

The Yellow Band is a distinct band of yellow limestone at 25,000 feet. Once up the initial steep 40-foot step, the terrain transforms from snow and ice to a gradual slope of loose, sedentary sandstone. Traversing this rocky section isn't technically difficult, but a fall from the Yellow Band is tantamount to death. It would be almost impossible to stop on this 2,000-foot, steep rock-ice slope.

———

On steep or dangerous ascents, climbers can clip onto the rope using two pieces of equipment, each one connected to their climbing harness via a nylon leash. One is a pear-shaped, metal loop with a lockable gate called a locking carabineer, and the other is a hand-held device called an ascender (or jumar). The ascender has a one-way locking mechanism so that it can be moved up a rope or locked in place when tension/weight is applied to it. In this way, a climber can literally hang on the rope or stop a fall. However, on relatively flat areas, like the main part of the Yellow Band, climbers usually unclip their ascenders so they can move along the rope more quickly.

———

After days of climbing up snow and ice, my crampons scraped and slid to find purchase on the Yellow Band's rocky surface. While the gradual incline allowed me to move faster, the narrow path and the loose rocks slowed me down. I also quickly became aware of one of the drawbacks of wearing an oxygen mask: it obstructed my already limited sight by blocking my ability to see the ground directly in front of and below me. I had to pay close attention to where I stepped, and even clipped onto the rope, this was no place to fall.

There were at least 30 people, maybe more, clipped onto the fixed rope on the traverse, and that presented several problems: traffic jams, passing climbers, and the potentially cumulative effect of someone falling. The rope was anchored to the rock-face at varying intervals (anywhere from 60 feet to 60 yards). At any one time, there were as many as five or more climbers clipped onto the rope between two anchors. If a climber fell, it could start a cascading event pulling other climbers clipped onto that section of rope off the mountain too. And to make matters worse, the weight and velocity of the falling climber(s) could rip the anchors right out of the wall, creating an even bigger tragedy.

———

On the Yellow Band there were a few places where two climbers could stand side-by-side, but most of the time we walked in single file. As I made my way across, I peered ahead and saw climbers bunching up in a couple of places. I thought it strange since I didn't see anything causing them to slow or stop. I wondered what was going on, and hoped there wasn't an accident or a climber suffering high-altitude problems.

I was about half way across the Yellow Band when I discovered a reason for the first bunch-up: some Sherpas were on their way down. There were so many climbers going for the summit, I had known it would only be a matter of time before we would run into people going the other direction. But passing on such an exposed, narrow area was dangerous. The mere thought made my heart beat faster, but these guys were moving so quickly that before I knew it, we were standing face-to-face.

———

The art of passing is a cooperative understanding between climbers using the eyes and the body to convey intent; no words are spoken. Highly experienced climbers are more comfortable passing and can pass without breaking stride. Less experienced climbers take more time to ensure that they are clipped onto something, even if it is just to the person next to them. And if there is a big difference in size between the climber trying to pass, the larger climber usually reaches around the smaller one, at least in theory.

———

As I neared the area of the second big bunch-up, I saw the reason why. We were approaching the Geneva Spur! Oh, I'd seen pictures of it, but pictures didn't do it justice! It was much more "impressive" in person, and was the final obstacle between me and Camp 4. I was up for the challenge, and thought, "Bring it on!"

At almost 26,000 feet, the Geneva Spur is an extremely exposed, steep wall of loose rock and ice, and a fall from it would end thousands of feet below at the base of the Lhotse Face. Luckily, there were two ropes leading up the wall, which allowed two sets of climbers to scale it at once, thus decreasing the wait time. It wasn't a technically difficult climb, but the extremely exposed location and loose rock-ice composition caused some climbers to take pause. As I stood near the base waiting for my turn, I watched the other climbers making their way up. The snowpack wasn't thick enough to cover the loose rocks and ice, and that made the ascent a bit more precarious for both the climbers and those waiting below. Falling rocks or ice could cause serious injury and even knock a climber off their feet, and the Geneva Spur was no place to lose your footing!

I should have felt anxious or at least nervous as I stood there waiting to start, but I was bewitched by the challenge and itching to go. Vivian was ahead of me and as I watched him head up, I felt a sudden surge of confidence and energy. I later found out that Bill had come up behind me and turned up my oxygen flow!

Vivian and me climbing the Geneva Spur nearing 26,000 feet. (Photo by Bill Allen)

I had so much fun, yes I said "fun," climbing the Geneva Spur that by the time I reached the top I was literally dancing in my crampons! Bill was standing next to me and told me to calm down and get my breathing under control, but I couldn't! I could see Camp 4 off in the distance, and I turned to Bill and said, "There's Camp 4, we're almost there!" He calmly replied, "Yes Cindy, I know."

———

In a daze of childlike wonder (no doubt thanks to the shortage of oxygen to my brain), I skipped through Camp 4 in search of my team. Skipping in crampons wasn't a smart thing to do, but I couldn't help myself. I'd done it! I was above 26,000 feet and the big, black pyramid of Everest with its long, white plume streaking across the sky was just off to my left! Fifty-one days after leaving home, I had reached Camp 4 along with what appeared to be about 140 other climbers.

Proudly holding the Vasculitis Foundation's banner at Camp 4 (26,100 ft). (Photo illustration by Bill Allen)

———

It was about 12:30 PM on May 22nd when we arrived at Everest's South Col and Camp 4, and the weather had been kind to us. The Jet Stream had moved slightly away and the cyclone was no longer headed directly for Everest, but there were still strong winds higher up the mountain. At that moment, they were considered "manageable," but they were predicted to increase the next day. The weather, however, wasn't our only concern; we also had to take into account the effect of the crowd.

All of the climbers at Camp 4 were struggling with the same decision – go or wait. Based on the weather, it was best to go that night, but with so many people poised for the summit, the traffic could produce dangerous, even deadly, consequences. A traffic jam on the rope could slow us to the point where we'd have to turn around and go back. If that happened, we would have no choice but to give up our only chance to summit. There was, however, a much worse scenario to consider. Even if we reached the summit, there was no guarantee that we could safely get down if other climbers were jamming the line. We could be completely prepared, supplied, and supported, and still end up trapped high on Everest where there is no hope of rescue and no safe harbor. Once we left Camp 4, we would be completely exposed to the whims of Mother Nature and the elements of Everest.

———

Scott and Bill struggled with the decision. We had enough oxygen and supplies to stay at Camp 4 for the night with the hope that the bulk of the other climbers would opt not to stay themselves. But if we waited the extra day, we risked losing our weather-window, and an additional night at Camp 4 wouldn't be pleasant.

———

At Camp 4, there is only 38% of the oxygen in each breath of air as compared to air at sea level, and the supplemental oxygen is just that, supplemental. It helps us to think more clearly, stay warmer, and delays some of the physiological effects of the extreme altitude. At this altitude, the amount of oxygen being carried by each red blood cell (oxygen saturation) is significantly reduced, and even with the supplemental oxygen, we are in a chronic state of hypoxia (oxygen deprivation). As the body tries to compensate for the lower level of oxygen, it shunts more blood to the brain, lungs, and other vital organs, and directs blood away from the digestive system and other unnecessary body functions.

Some other physiological concerns include severe fatigue to the point that we can't get ourselves back down the mountain; hypothermia which can lead to unconsciousness and death; frostbite where the skin and underlying tissues freeze; the development of Acute Mountain Sickness (AMS) or High Altitude Cerebral Edema (HACE), both of which cause swelling of the brain; and High Altitude Pulmonary Edema (HAPE) where fluid accumulates in the lungs. There's a reason why this extreme altitude is referred to as the "Death Zone." It's a place where humans cannot survive; we are only allowed a very short visit.

———

After my excitement subsided, I knew that I had to call Larry and let him know that I had made it safely to Camp 4. It was the middle of the night back home, but I knew Larry would be worried if he didn't hear from me. I got the satellite phone and went inside my tent, but there was no way to make a call without removing my gloves and oxygen mask, and I was already feeling the compounding effects of fatigue and hypoxia, further impeding my cognitive function. After getting out my glasses and changing the SIM card, I dialed the first number that appeared. It was Rob Strauss, a producer from Southern California Public Radio, who had been covering my story with Alex Cohen of *All Things Considered*. The call went through to his voice mail and I left a message that I was at Camp 4. For some reason I started to cry as I asked him to call Larry and tell him that I was "okay." I also told Rob to tell Larry that he wouldn't hear from me if we went for the summit, but not to worry because no news was good news. Looking back, I find it hard to believe that I called Rob instead of Larry, but my fingers were numb and I was so tired that hitting the redial button was all I could manage at the time, and to this day I regret that choice.

———

Finally the decision was made. We were leaving for the summit at 9 PM! With only a few hours to eat, drink, and rest, I snapped out of my mindless lethargy, and focused. I started going down my mental checklist. I had two half-liter water bottles that would go in the front chest pockets of my down suit along with my camera, two packets of energy gel (liquid food), the NORD banner, family photos, and my medicine. I packed my backpack with my summit mittens, goggles, a liter of water, two more energy gels, sunscreen, and a small first-aid kit. I had very little time left, and I wanted to take a nap, if that was even possible, but I had to eat something first. So I reached into my zip-lock bag and took out the special food I had brought from home and saved for this very moment. It was lightweight, full of calories, and the one thing I was certain I'd be able to eat. Cross-legged, I sat in my tent munching on my magic mountain food – Cheetos.

Chapter 14

BUT I WOULD NOT BE ALONE

Perhaps love is like a resting place, a shelter from the storm

It exists to give you comfort, it is there to keep you warm

And in those times of trouble when you are most alone

The memory of love will bring you home

Perhaps love is like the mountains, full of conflict, full of change

Like a fire when it's cold outside, thunder when it rains

If I should live forever, and all my dreams come true

My memories of love will be of you

(PERHAPS LOVE by John Denver)

The moment for which I had worked so hard, waited so long, and suffered so much was now at hand. I was about to journey into one of the world's most hostile, unforgiving environments, but I wouldn't be alone. Larry and Teshia's pictures were in the chest pocket of my down suit, close to my heart.

———

I woke to the sound of Bill's voice, "Cindy, hot chocolate or soup?" I sat up, pulled off my oxygen mask, closed the flow valve, and replied, "Soup." I inch-wormed down to the door of my tent still in my sleeping bag, and as I opened the zipper I heard, "No soup," and a hand poked into the tent holding a packet of hot chocolate. I took the packet and stuck my cup through the opening. Bill filled it with hot water, a precious commodity, and I said, "Thanks," as he walked toward the next tent. I knew I wouldn't be eating again for a long time, so I added some Cheetos to my pre-summit dinner menu. Hot chocolate and Cheetos – my Mt. Everest summit fuel.

———

I can only describe the feeling of being at Camp 4 as surreal. In this isolated, deadly, desolate place, it was as if I was no longer on our planet. Maybe this was what it was like to be on the moon. It felt like I existed outside of myself; I was there, but I wasn't.

———

I looked at my watch, it was 7 PM. We had two hours before we were scheduled to leave, and I knew it would pass in an instant! I was surprised and relieved that I had gotten some sleep. I don't know if it was 20 minutes or two hours, but however much I got, it helped. I had been awake since 3 AM and over the last 16 hours I'd climbed from Camp 3 to Camp 4, and was now packing to climb to the summit. I knew it was going to be a long time until I returned to this tent and my sleeping bag. Under the best conditions, the round-trip summit climb would take me about 12 hours, but the sheer number of other climbers attempting to summit was going to significantly affect that timeline. I just didn't know to what degree.

———

We stepped out of Camp 4 at 9 PM. It was cold and dark, but not windy. After crossing a short, gradually sloping section, we reached the fixed rope. I clipped on behind Scott, my climbing Sherpa clipped on behind me, and we started up. Our next stop was The Balcony at 27,600 feet.

With the exception of a dozen or so tricky parts, the climb to The Balcony was steep but not technically difficult. Still the pace on the rope was painfully slow, and at times, the line would completely stop. A few climbers got so frustrated that they unclipped and went up alongside the line, but that was risky, especially in the dark. Everyone else just stood there and waited for the line to move. I'd probably been climbing for about an hour when I looked behind me. Wow! For as many climbers as there were ahead, there were at least twice as many behind. Thank goodness we'd gotten an early start.

I turned and looked back up the mountain, wondering what was there. It was so dark that the only thing I could see was a single, shimmering line of twinkling headlamps, as if someone had strung a giant string of Christmas lights from the South Summit. Hour after hour, I watched this shining snake slowly wriggle up the mountain as I fell into a hypnotic rhythm of stepping, breathing, clipping, and unclipping. Funny how hypoxia affects brain.

The closer we got to The Balcony, the more technical spots we had to tackle. I knew when I was nearing one because the line would slow to a stop. In the darkness, I wasn't able to see exactly what it was, but I could judge its difficulty by how long it took others to clear it. By the time I was within sight of the obstacle, I would observe how the climbers ahead of me made their way over the section. Sometimes watching them helped, and if not, I'd do it "Cindy Style," and crawl, scrape, and scramble up or over anyway I could. It may not have been pretty, but it worked.

As I continued up, I saw two men sitting just to the left of the rope, and as I passed them, I overheard one of the men talking to a third climber. He said that this was as far as they were going, and that after a short rest, they were heading down. WOW! I'd expected to see people aborting the summit and turning around, but I didn't expect to see it so soon.

Within minutes I discovered why the two men had stopped: a very difficult section that began with a scramble up a rock wall that smoothed out into slabs near the top. I took a deep breath, and started up. I scrambled high enough so that I could grab the top edge, but my legs were too short to reach the next foothold. I had to use my arms. As I pulled myself up toward the top of the lip, I was abruptly stopped in place by my own carabineer. It had become wedged in a crack and I was stuck in a very uncomfortable position! With so many climbers weighting the rope, it was pulled so tightly against the slab that it might as well have been part of it. I wasn't able to get enough slack to free my carabineer, and decided it was time for "Plan B." I looked at the rope on the top of the slab to see if I might be able to clip onto it. If so, it would allow me to unclip my jammed lower carabineer. I reached up and tugged on the rope. Nope, the upper rope was just as tight against the slab.

I only had one option left. I was going to have to simultaneously pull myself and my carabineer over the lip. I grabbed the edge of the lip with one hand and my carabineer with the other, and in a burst of strength, I pulled my body up while dragging my carabineer up the crack in the rock. I managed to get high enough to swing my body onto the edge, but my jammed carabineer prevented me from getting completely over the lip. I had to free it, and myself, so I sprawled across the slab in some contorted position so I could use both hands to move my carabineer. I reached down and got a firm grip on my carabineer with one hand, and grabbed the rope with my other. Using my body as a fulcrum, I worked the carabineer to the edge of the lip and with a final burst of energy, I lifted the rope that one-third of an inch I needed to get my carabineer over. I was finally free, and off I went. It was all just part of the adventure.

———

We climbed onto The Balcony, a small platform at 27,600 feet, at around 1 AM. It had taken us four hours to get there, and when I arrived, there were already about 20 people squeezed into a huddled mass on the space the size of two pool tables, and more were coming. It was crazy! Climbers, Sherpas, backpacks, and oxygen bottles took up every available inch. And on The Balcony, no one was clipped onto a rope. If someone slipped or was bumped, they'd disappear off the edge and into the darkness.

As our Sherpas retrieved our new oxygen bottles, we had a few minutes to rest, have a snack, and drink some water. I had to remove my mask in order to eat or drink, and at that altitude, I wanted oxygen more than food or water, but I knew better. I took off my outer glove, reached into my pocket, and pulled out my water bottle. I needed to drink when I could. This was only the beginning of what was sure to be a long, difficult day.

———

After getting a full oxygen bottle, I left The Balcony and headed up the Southeast Ridge. Within minutes of leaving, I knew something was wrong with my oxygen mask. I checked the flow indicator first; the oxygen was flowing. Next, I checked the hose, and as far as I could tell, there was no problem there. So I checked the intake connection and the exhaust valve, and everything seemed fine. But I knew it wasn't. I continued climbing anyway.

The hours passed as I ascended into the darkness, ever upward. With the exception of Everest, there are only four mountain peaks higher than The Balcony: Makalu at 27,765 feet, Lhotse at 27,890 feet, Kangchenjunga at 28,169 feet, and K2 at 28,253 feet. By now I was surely higher than Makalu and Lhotse, and I had to be nearing the height of the other two.

Soon, I would be climbing on a place that was higher than anywhere else in the world – a place few have been.

———

From this point, my memory fades in and out of focus. There are times when I can recall every detail, and then there are, what feel like, gaps in time. I'm really not sure if it's just that as the hours passed, nothing changed or if I really lost some moments. Maybe I have complete recollection and the confusion is caused by the pictures in my mind. Maybe those snapshots are so similar that I simply can't distinguish one from another. I'll never know.

———

As we crossed a wide, moderately sloped section, the pace on the line slowed to an agonizing crawl. At times, I stood in one place for 15 to 20 minutes before taking the next step – one step! Time was moving, but we were not! While I slowly made my way up the slope, the sky began to take on a pink hue. The sun was rising. Of all the sights in this world, I can say that standing at almost 28,500 feet and watching the sun peak up over the snow-capped Himalayans was the most beautiful thing I'd ever seen. I'll admit that my brain was starved for oxygen, but I believe that my hard work and perseverance was rewarded with the opportunity to watch this magnificent sight. It was truly magical.

Now that the sun was up, I could see what was causing the big problem on the line: about 200 feet ahead was the first of several steep, rock-faces. One by one the climbers worked their way up the rocky face, sending rocks and ice showering down on the waiting climbers. I spent the next hour watching for falling objects, some the size of dinner plates!

As the climbers before me slowly picked their way up the rock-face, a pattern quickly emerged. There was one section where some climbers would just stop, afraid to make the next move. When that happened, a Sherpa, guide, or another climber would somehow manage to get the climber up. The line had to keep moving; the clock was ticking.

———

Finally, it was my turn. As I approached the base of the wall, I saw several old ropes hanging down the rock-face, their loose ends curled up on the snow like a nest of multicolored snakes waiting to strike. I circled this crampon-snagging snare and carefully made my way over to this year's red rope and clipped on. The rock was very loose, and as hard as I tried, I couldn't climb without pieces breaking off. I'd yell, "Rock" to warn the climbers below. It seemed like the previous climbers should have knocked away all the loose rocks. We'd spent hours dodging them. How could there be more?

The lower section of the wall wasn't difficult, but then I came to the spot that had stopped the other climbers, and I could see why! There was a four-foot gap in the wall and to cross it, I was going to have to unclip from the line, jump up and over the gap, and land on a loose, rocky edge. It had to be done. So, I unclipped and sprang up and across the gap. With hands grasping and crampons scraping, I found purchase on the small platform. By this point, these leaps-of-faith were just part of the day's climb.

The fun, however, didn't end with that jump. Once across and sure of my footing, I walked over, clipped back onto the rope, and looked up at the next section – a steep, 80-degree, loose-rock wall. I stood there for a few minutes planning my route. Fortunately, and unfortunately, I had to stay within the range of the rope, which restricted me to a section where, once again, the first step was higher than my leg could reach.

171

Dang these short legs! After several minutes trying to get onto the step, I switched to looking for handholds. Wearing my big, black gloves, I pawed at the rock but found nothing. So, I clipped my ascender onto the rope, and using my arms, pulled myself up the rock-face. Again, it wasn't pretty, but it worked, and I was up.

Before long, I was standing at the base of another rock wall. I was very high, as in altitude, and functioning on a more instinctive level. Thank goodness for all that training! There was no more wasting time. I got out my ascender and scrambled to the top of the wall. After taking a few steps, I looked up in anticipation of the next section. It took a few seconds for my brain to register what my eyes were seeing. Oh my gosh! I was just below the South Summit of Mt. Everest, and I could clearly see the Hillary Step and Everest's familiar white plume blowing across the sky. Wow! It looked just like the pictures!

———

At the risk of sounding delusional or insulting, I must say that at that point, it was almost impossible to tell the identity of individual climbers. During the long night and day of climbing, it didn't really make a difference, but as I approached an extremely dangerous section of the climb, I wanted to know who was around me. Who was that person ahead of me? What about that person behind? And who was that trying to pass!?! I knew my team, but I didn't know these other climbers, and I wanted to keep my distance. Accidents happened too easily on Everest.

Almost all of the climbers were wearing one of three or four types of red, orange, or yellow-colored down suits. Add goggles and an oxygen mask, and the person's identity, even if known, was difficult to discern. Scott and Bill had foreseen this situation and had made reflective name tags for every member of the team, including our Sherpas. We all wore a reflector tied around our upper arm, and another one attached to our back-packs. Even if I couldn't tell who the person was, I'd at least know that they were on my team.

———

I headed toward the South Summit. I knew Scott and Ania were somewhere not too far ahead, but to my surprise, it was Bill's voice I heard. I looked to my left and there he was, standing just off the trail. Where had he come from? Bill stopped me and asked, "Cindy, do you know how much energy it's going to take to get to the summit and all the way back down?" I thought for a moment and then said, "Yes." Bill nodded and I walked on.

I continued up the snow slope and over to the small hump called the South Summit. This was where we were to switch-out our oxygen. I headed for a narrow area where I could sit and stay clipped to the line without blocking other climbers trying to pass. As I approached, I saw Ania, but she was al-ready up and on her way, and after getting my fresh oxygen bottle, I followed. I was at 28,700 feet, and it felt like it.

As I walked, I recognized Scott standing off to the side. He and another person (maybe Bill) were talking to a female climber sitting in the snow. I didn't know who she was, but I could tell she was having some kind of problem. As I went by, I overheard something about "a broken toe," and "It's two and a half hours round trip back to here." I felt bad for her, but I had to refocus my attention. I was approaching the world's highest, razor-edged ridge – the Cornice Traverse!

The Cornice Traverse and the Hillary Step with the wind creating Mt. Everest's famous white plume. (Photo by Bill Allen)

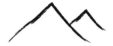

Chapter 15

BEYOND IMAGINATION

The Cornice Traverse was akin to walking across the knife-edge of the world. It was a very narrow, extremely exposed, 300-foot horizontal ridge of rock, snow, and ice. At just below 29,000 feet, it was the passageway to the top of the world. A rope was anchored to the west-facing slope and a narrow path had been worn into the side. There was a 10,000-foot drop-off to the right, and an 8,000-foot drop-off to the left. Either way, an unarrested fall meant certain death. And if the thought of crossing this razor-edged ridge wasn't imposing enough, what was waiting on the other side certainly was – the infamous Hillary Step.

Before starting across I looked down to see what was, or more precisely, what wasn't there. In the event that I fell and stayed attached to the rope, I wanted a mental picture to help me climb back up, if that was even possible. If I fell and didn't stay attached, it wouldn't matter. After this brief survey I never looked down again. As I stood waiting for my turn to cross, a cold wind stung my face. The wind was picking up and coming in from the East, the direction of the approaching cyclone.

It was finally my turn. I clipped onto the rope and stepped into the frozen footsteps of those who had gone before me. I focused solely on what was directly ahead: the location of the next anchor and the odd bits of old rope to avoid. I paid special attention to my foot placement. When I was about half way across, two climbers approached from the opposite direction, and I thought, "here we go!" We were going to have to pass, but as it turned out, this particular spot wasn't bad relatively speaking, and we safely passed each other at 29,000 feet.

I had been so focused on each step, that before I realized it, I found myself standing in a queue of climbers waiting to go up the Hillary Step. It had looked intimidating from a distance with its extremely exposed, steep rock-ice face decorated with a seemingly stationary line of multicolored down suits. But as I stood at the base, watching the climbers ahead of me make their way up, the first 15 feet looked surprisingly manageable – a moderately-steep section of mixed rock and snow. Unbelievable, I was about to climb the Hillary Step!

———

The famed Hillary Step was a 40-foot spur of rock, snow, and ice. People were moving slowly and carefully as they climbed, and while I couldn't see them all, I knew there were at least 20 climbers ahead of me. I was stuck in a high-altitude traffic jam on the most difficult section of Everest's south side. After waiting for the climbers ahead of me to go up, and three others to come down, I got started. The first few feet were on snow, but soon my crampons were scraping against rock as I made my way up from the base and onto a small platform. I was stopped by more climbers coming down, and while I waited I looked up to see what exciting bit of climbing was next, and what I saw was electrifying! A dozen climbers were working their way up a maze-like wall of rocks, boulders, and ice. WOW! Game on!

I switched into my *10-feet-at-a-time* mode and continued up. In a hypoxic state of sheer determination, I spent the next however-long scrambling up, over, around, and across rocks, snow, and ice as I made my way toward the summit. I eventually came to a rock-bulge that stuck out over the 8,000-foot drop and I was going to have to straddle it to cross it, though I couldn't see what was on the other side. The Sherpa in front of me went around it, and vanished. I figured he had to be somewhere, so I hugged the rock and stretched out my left leg until it touched something solid. Then shifting my weight onto that leg, I tried to bring my other leg around, but it was stuck, wedged in the rocks. After a bit of twisting, shifting, and maneuvering, I freed my leg and cleared the rock. Spotting the missing Sherpa, I continued on. This was the way of the Hillary Step.

As abruptly as it had started, it ended. I cleared the final rock section and looked up at the slope leading to the summit of Mt. Everest. I had less than 1,000 feet to walk and I would be standing on the top of the world! I stood for a minute assessing my physical and mental condition. I had been climbing for days with almost no sleep and very little to eat. I was near 29,000 feet where every breath of air contained only 33% oxygen, and I had just completed the wildest climb of my life. I wanted to make sure my legs and brain were in proper working order. I hadn't come this far only to plummet off the side of the mountain because I was a bit shaky.

I slowly continued up the snow slope. My legs felt strong and steady and my mind seemed clear (at least to me). As I walked toward the summit, I looked around. The view was amazing, beautiful, fantastic! There are no words to accurately describe what I saw or how I felt. It was as if I could see the entire world in one glance. I was looking down at the tops of some of the world's highest mountains, and after a few more steps, I would be higher than everything on Earth!

———

As I walked toward the summit, I felt my elation being eclipsed by something else. What? Was my oxygen flowing?

Yes, but something wasn't right. What was it? Slowly I began to feel a sense of anxiety come over me. I was almost at the top of the world, but the closer I got, the more anxious I became. Then I realized what was going on: there were more than 25 people between me and the summit, most of them strangers, and that translated to one thing – unpredictable danger!

A crowd on the top of the world! (Photo by Bill Allen)

I was relieved to see Ania and some of our Sherpas standing off to the side. I began walking toward them but changed my mind, and headed for the colorful prayer-flags crowning the summit. At 9:02 AM on May 23, 2010, I stepped onto the top of the world. After years of hardship and training, I was finally standing on the summit of Mt. Everest, but to my surprise, I wasn't happy.

I'd seen pictures showing the size of the summit, but in person, it was shockingly small. I was standing in a crowd of climbers from all over the world on the space the size of a pool table! After more than 7 weeks of climbing, acclimatizing, waiting, and wondering, we had all made it. In a state of excited abandon, many cheered and jumped in celebration, but their exuberance made me extremely nervous. An accidental bump or whack of an arm could send me off the mountain and I would just disappear. Gone!

Every fiber in my body told me to get away from the celebrating crowd, so I left the summit and walked a few feet down the slope. There, I dug my crampon-spikes into the hard, wind-blown snow and sat down. I'd made it to the summit — fantastic. But that feeling of anxiety kept nipping at me, telling me to leave, that I wasn't supposed to be here. Before I left though, I needed to get a picture of me holding the NORD banner, and I had to take my pills. Scott walked up and asked how I was. I said "fine," and asked him to take a picture of me. I took out my camera, handed it to him, and hoped that it would work in this extreme environment. Then I reached into my pocket and took out the banner, but it was so windy that I almost lost hold of it. No way! That banner had to be in my summit photo; together we were a symbol of hope. So to make sure I wouldn't lose it, I removed one glove, grabbed the banner, and held it out in front of me. Scott snapped two pictures and handed my camera back to me. I quickly replaced my glove and stuffed the banner and camera into my pocket. I had my summit picture. But I still needed to take my pills, and now, my fingers were numb.

Me holding the National Organization of Rare Disorders Banner at 29,035 feet! (Photo by Scott Woolums)

My teammates, Paul and Denise, walked up and sat down a few feet below me. They turned and asked if I would take a picture of them holding their banner. I told them that I couldn't because my fingers were already painfully cold. I felt bad not being able to help them out, but I knew that just a few minutes of extreme cold exposure could cause frostbite, and I still needed to take my medication.

I was sitting on a steep slope, afraid that if I took my water bottle and pills out, my numb fingers would drop them off the side of the mountain. So I got up and moved down about 15 feet to a more level spot. Once seated, I pulled both bottles out of my pocket, but in order to take my pills out of their small protective container, I had to remove my glove again. Great! It had been over 12 hours since I last took my medication, and I still had to climb who-knows how many hours to get back down to Camp 4. I had to take my pills now.

After fumbling around for several minutes, I managed to take my meds, drink some water, and squeeze a packet of energy gel into my mouth. The only food I'd eaten since leaving Camp 4 was two energy gels totaling 300 calories, though I had probably burned about 8,000 calories over the past 12 hours alone. That was more than I'd burn at home over the course of three or four days, and I still had to climb back down. But eating was not one of my priorities. In fact, it was pretty much pointless. I knew at this altitude my body was dining on itself. It was much more efficient to break down my own tissues to fuel my body than it was to try and digest food. It was actually much more important to drink something because dehydration could cause many altitude-related problems, and as incredible as this may sound, with the exception of my fingers, all things considered, physically I felt fine.

———

It was sunny on the summit, but I could see a white haze moving in from the east. The wind was growing stronger, and I was getting colder from not moving. It was time to start down. I got up and was walking toward the group when I ran into Paul. He asked me if I had the satellite phone, and I told him that I didn't have the phone, but I did have a super SIM card. I asked him if he wanted it, but he declined.

Before I left home I had purchased a special SIM card that was supposed to work from the summit. My original plan was to call Larry when I reached the summit, but my fingers couldn't manage switching the tiny SIM cards or pushing the buttons on the phone. They were completely numb, and for the most part, useless. The only thing I could feel from my fingers was pain. I walked over to the head climbing Sherpa and told him that I was going down. The longer I stayed, the colder I got, and the weather was changing for the worse. I had to get out of there.

As I turned to head down, I saw more climbers coming up and one of them was my teammate, Vivian! I went over to him and we gave each other the biggest hug, a hug that embodied all of the work and hardship we had overcome to earn the privilege of standing on the top of the world. I looked through his goggles and into his eyes and saw that they were beaming with joy, happiness in its purest form, a feeling so fleeting, so rare, that many live a lifetime without knowing its wonder.

I was so overwhelmed by Vivian's joy that I almost started to cry, but I had to get off the summit, so I checked my emotions, and through my oxygen mask yelled "congratulations" to Vivian, and turned to head down. Without looking back, I started down the slope toward the Hillary Step. I was relieved to know that everyone in our group had made it to the summit and appeared well, but we still had a long way to go before we could begin to think about relaxing.

As I started down the top section of the Hillary Step, I noticed that my vision was getting blurry. I stopped and checked to see if my glasses were fogged-up (a common problem). They were a little foggy so I cleaned them and continued down. But my vision kept getting worse and it wasn't due to fogged-up glasses. Why I couldn't see?

———

I had experienced something similar, but to a much lesser degree, several weeks earlier while climbing the Lhotse Face on our last rotation. At that time, the blurriness in my vision had only lasted for a few minutes, but it had concerned me enough to take a trip to the Everest ER once we had returned to Base Camp. I had described what happened to Dr. Hackett, and although he couldn't be certain, he thought he had an idea as to the cause of my blurred vision. Dr. Hackett explained that when cold wind blows on the corneas – they freeze.

———

Oh my gosh! I had frozen corneas at 29,000 feet! By the time I realized what was happening, I only had about 30% of my vision left, and I was going down the Hillary Step! I told my climbing Sherpa that I couldn't see and he helped me rappel down a short, steep section of rock. The rest of the way, I used the rope as a guide, clipping and unclipping, stumbling my way down the Hillary Step. I reached the bottom of the Step and was about a third of the way across the Cornice Traverse when two climbers approached from the opposite direction. They were on their way up, and unlike the last time I had to pass climbers on the ridge, we were not in a safe section to do so. But they were late and in a hurry, so the first climber unclipped from the rope and climbed up and over me, very close to the cornice lip. It was an extremely dangerous move that his fellow climber wasn't willing to take, so he literally started to climb me! I dug in my crampons and leaned into the slope, trying to gain as much purchase as possible. He made it past me and continued on, as did I.

In the confusion, my Sherpa had gotten ahead of me on the line, but even with my limited vision, as long as the climbing wasn't technical, I could keep moving by following the rope. I caught up to my climbing Sherpa just below the South Summit. He was busy loading used oxygen bottles. As I waited, Bill came by and asked me if something was wrong. I told him that I was having trouble with my vision. I could see shapes and contrast, but I had no depth perception. Bill clipped onto the rope in front of me and we started down the snow slope that led to the first steep rock-face. But all of those people who had been on the summit were now going down too, and that created a huge line of waiting climbers that stretched from the top of the rock-face all the way up the slope. So we sat perched on the slope and waited. Every 10 or 15 minutes we'd get up and move another 10 or 15 feet; then we'd sit and wait again. It was cold and windy, and sitting around, not moving made it worse, but we were gradually getting closer to the top of the rock-face.

After about 45 minutes I reached the wall, but I couldn't see to rappel down. I was actually quite comfortable with rappelling and I knew that I didn't need to see, that my arms and legs would do the work and get me down. I was set up and in position, but I just couldn't force myself over that first lip. My brain was telling me to just lean back and go, but I couldn't. Bill was hanging off an anchor to my left, and he said, "Cindy, you're getting off this mountain!" He reached out, grabbed my backpack, and plucked me off the rock. Perfect! I was free and on my way down. Bill landed next to me. Smiling, I thanked him for the "pluck."

By the time we got to the next rock-face, the storm had reached us. This time Bill wasn't wasting any time, and after I had set up for the rappel, he sent me on my way. Once down the rock-faces, I could climb on my own. Following the rope and the shapes of the other climbers, I made my way to the top of the narrow, snow ridge that led down to The Balcony, but again, there was a bottle-neck of climbers. Coming up the night before, we had easily crossed it, but now the storm had created near white-out conditions with snow and wind hitting us at about 35 to 40 MPH. Still, it shouldn't have caused this kind of back up.

It soon became apparent that the problem wasn't on the ridge; it was below at The Balcony. Too many climbers were staying on the small platform so there wasn't room for us to come down. Why weren't those climbers going down? The conditions were bad, but it was only going to get worse, and the climbers on The Balcony weren't the only ones not descending, the climbers on the rope in front of us weren't budging either. It looked like someone was acting as a gatekeeper and only allowing six climbers to cross the ridge at one time. I didn't know who the person was or whether or not all of the climbers were in the same group, and I didn't care. Whatever was going on, time was up and we were coming down.

Once we got to The Balcony we discovered the source of the traffic jam. There was a group of climbers huddled over someone lying on the snow. Scott went over to investigate. The climber had some form of altitude sickness and he was in bad shape. The group needed help to get the man down, so Scott loaned them one of our Sherpas and gave them some oxygen.

———

After getting a fresh oxygen bottle, I left The Balcony for the long climb down to Camp 4. It had taken four hours to climb up this section, but it should be much faster going down. I'd been above 26,000 feet for over 26 hours, and climbing for more than 16. I was mentally and physically exhausted.

Between the wind, the snow, and my vision, it was difficult to see where my next step would take me. I could differentiate dark from light, thus rock from snow, so if I was approaching a dark section, I assumed it was rock. And if the ground was lighter in color, I knew I was approaching snow, ice or a drop-off. This type of situation was much trickier because I had no depth perception. I never knew if the next step would drop two inches, two feet, or more. I'd have to assess each step using the location of anchors, the angle of the rope, and the pitch of the rocks. Although I was exhausted, my arms were still strong and my best chance of stopping a fall was to use a technique called the arm-wrap. Standing with my back to the rope, I would wrap the rope around my lower arm, run it up under my armpit, across my backpack, and hold onto the upper section of rope with my other hand. I fell countless times as I descended, but I didn't care. I maintained my grip on the rope and landed on my behind. The only thing that mattered was getting down the mountain.

At one point Vivian came up from behind me and we walked and talked for a while. With Vivian on the rope in front of me, I could move much faster, but after a while we separated, and I continued down alone. The ground was becoming more rocky and level, so I looked up to see what I was approaching, and in the hazy distance, I could make out colored tents. I'd been so focused on each individual step that I hadn't noticed that I was almost back to Camp 4.

———

Smiling, I stepped out of my opaque obscurity and walked toward our tents. It was like waking from a dream, a long, cold, crazy dream. As soon as I got to the second tent, a Sherpa's arm popped out holding a cup of hot lemon tea. I thanked him as I took the cup, walked a few more feet, and plopped to the ground. I'd done it! I'd made it down! I had summited Mt. Everest and was safely back at Camp 4.

Holding the cup in my big, black gloves, I just sat there, unmoving. It felt so good just to be, and nothing more. After a few minutes, I pulled off my oxygen mask, removed my pack, and drank the tea. It was the first thing I'd had to eat or drink since the summit. I wasn't sure how long ago that had been, so I got up, walked over to Scott and asked him the time. He said, "4:30." WOW! It had taken us 18.5 hours to go from Camp 4 to the summit and back. 18.5 hours!

———

The storm was getting stronger and I needed to rest. I handed the empty cup to the Sherpa, grabbed my pack, and headed for my tent. I unzipped the door, threw in my pack, and quickly zipped it back up. The wind was blowing snow directly inside. I took off my crampons and buried them in the snow nearby, and after removing my harness, I climbed into my tent. I pulled off my outer boots and stuck them in the corner along with my harness. Between the snow on me and my gear, and the snow that had blown in, I could have made a snowman inside my tent. Using my mittens, I gathered the snow into a pile, unzipped a small opening, and shoveled out as much of it as I could. The rest I swept into the other corner. Having some snow inside the tent wasn't a problem because it would never get warm enough for it to melt.

———

After spending so long exposed to the ravages of the mountain, it felt strange to be in my tent with my sleeping bag and my stuff, what little of it there was. Sure, I was still over 26,000 feet with a storm blowing outside, but all things considered, for the moment, I was safe.

———

I grabbed my big, blue sleeping bag and crawled inside. What next? Pills. I reached inside my down suit and pulled out my smaller water bottles. One was empty, but the other one was still half full. That meant I had only drunk three-fourths of a liter of water during the past 18.5 hours, and that was not good. I took my pills, finished the rest of the water, and decided that it was time to free my feet, which had been inside my boot-liners for over 20 hours. I untied the laces and pulled off the liners. The cold air hit my sock-covered feet instantly, and for a few brief seconds felt good, but I knew better and quickly stuck my feet back inside my sleeping bag. I started to put my liners in too, but I still had some other things to do and it was difficult to move around with a lot of stuff inside the bag. So I placed the boot-liners next to my sleeping bag. I'd put them in later, when I was ready to lie down.

It was starting to get dark and already very cold, but once the sun went down, it was going to get considerably colder. I was working to get everything organized, making sure that the items I'd need during the night were close enough for me to reach without having to leave the relative warmth of my sleeping bag. As the light faded from the sky, I dug out my headlamp and checked the tent for any last items that needed to go inside my sleeping bag; anything left out would be frozen solid by morning.

I was amazed that I was still able to function, but what little energy I had left was quickly waning, and I still had to eat. I lay down, opened a package of cheese-and-crackers, and tried to eat, but I was so dehydrated that the cracker just stuck to the inside of my mouth. I didn't have any saliva to moisten it, let alone swallow. I reached into my sleeping bag and pulled out the one-liter water bottle that I had carried inside my backpack. With the exception of its thermal case, the bottle had been exposed to the cold since we had left for the summit. Expecting it to be frozen, I had put it in my sleeping bag to melt during the night. But I needed water now so I opened it, and to my surprise, it was still liquid. I just had to punch through an inch-thick layer of ice sealing the bottle opening, so I got out my knife.

By that point, I had been off my oxygen for a while and was starting to feel dizzy. The tent was secured, I'd taken my pills, I had eaten, and my gear and water bottles were in my sleeping bag. I grabbed my pack and pulled out the oxygen bottle and my mask. I had known something was wrong with my oxygen mask since first leaving The Balcony on the way to the summit, but I had been unable to find the problem. I checked it again more thoroughly, but still couldn't find anything wrong, and I was spent. I nestled the oxygen bottle in between my sleeping bag and another oxygen bottle. We were finishing up the partially used bottles, and at some point during the night, I would have to wake up and switch to the other bottle.

———

I had just experienced the most difficult day of my life. I was exhausted beyond any level I had ever known or could have imagined. I tried to convince myself to get dressed, go over and get the satellite phone, and call Larry. I knew Scott or Bill had called Todd, and Todd would spread the word of our successful summit and safe return to Camp 4. But I needed to call Larry and it was incomprehensible that I wouldn't; I just couldn't. Larry, please forgive me.

———

After reaching the summit and returning safely back to Camp 4 I had expected to feel a sense of relief, but I didn't. I was still at over 26,000 feet in a place not meant for humans. We were leaving for Camp 2 in the morning, but I knew that

I wouldn't be able to relax or celebrate until we are all off this mountain and safely back at Base Camp. There were still several days of work and danger ahead, and this was neither the time nor place to let my guard down.

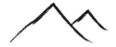

Chapter 16

MY MISTAKE

There was no whisper, no wind, just a nebulous of bright orange light. My eyes were open yet unseeing. How odd. Was I awake within my own dream? As I lay there unmoving, awareness eluded me. Slowly my eyes began to focus and I felt the coldness of the air. It was morning.

A fog of fatigue eclipsed my mind, and my listless body rebelled against my efforts to move. I blinked my eyes in an attempt to regain some level of cognizance when I was suddenly catapulted into consciousness. During the night, the storm had blown into my tent and covered everything with snow. Really! And as if that wasn't bad enough, I'd been so utterly exhausted that I had fallen asleep without putting my big gloves or boot-liners in my sleeping bag!

I sat up and looked at my oxygen gauge – empty. Of course it was. So I took off my mask and set it aside. How could I have been so careless!?! Now I had to salvage what I could. Carefully I reached down and shook the snow off of my sleeping bag toward the bottom of the tent. Then, while still inside the bag, I inch-wormed onto my knees so I could uncover the rest of my gear. I saw my pack and climbing harness, but I couldn't see my gloves or boot-liners. I needed to get them inside my sleeping bag as soon as possible. My body heat was trapped in the bag, and with luck, it would help to thaw them. If not, I could lose some fingers or toes, or both!

I found my boot-liners next to me. Luckily they had been under my bag and weren't frozen. I stuffed them into my sleeping bag and started searching for my gloves. I knew where they should have been, but they weren't there. Where were my gloves? I finally found them under my pack next to the side of the tent and they were frozen stiff! I spent several minutes massaging them until they became more pliable. Then I stuck the gloves into my bag. It was so cold inside my tent, I seriously doubted that I would be able to generate enough body heat to warm them, but I had to try. Finally, I grabbed my outer-boot shells, shook the snow out of them, and then off of the rest of my stuff, and piled everything next to me. It was not a good beginning to the day.

Breathless and unnerved by the situation, I lay back down and pulled my sleeping bag up and around my head trying to trap every bit of heat. I had just gotten the bag zipped around my face when I realized that I hadn't taken my medicine. Staying cocooned inside my bag, I reached into the pockets of my down suit, and pulled out my water bottle and pills. After taking my medication I had to wait an hour before I could eat anything, so I just lay there scolding myself for making such a serious mistake.

———

As I waited, I glanced over at my oxygen mask. I still hadn't figured out what was wrong with it. I reached over and picked it up, and in the light of day, I immediately discovered the problem. The exhaust valve was coming off! I knew something had happened to my mask at The Balcony on my way to the summit. There were so many climbers on that small platform, all jostling and bumping into each other, something or someone must have hit my valve and broken it. Wow! I had climbed from The Balcony to the summit and back to Camp 4 with some of the oxygen flowing out of my mask instead of into my lungs! How much oxygen had I lost? Was that why I felt such anxiety on the summit? Well, the mystery was solved, and at this point, what had happened was irrelevant. What was relevant was getting down the mountain.

———

The winds had calmed and the sun was up. It was time to pack the tents and descend to Camp 2. My boot-liners had been on for about 30 minutes, and though still cold, my feet had warmed them up some. My big gloves, on the other hand, were soaking wet and freezing, so I put on my medium-weight gloves, and planned to switch to the big ones later.

The face of the Geneva Spur was several hundred yards below Camp 4. On the way up we had to climb the icy, rock spur, but going down we could rappel. Thankfully, my corneas had thawed during the night, and once again, I was completely comfortable rappelling. I stepped over to the anchor, set up my equipment, and was off. By the time I got down the Spur and onto the Yellow Band, my feeling of comfort had dissolved into the myopic obscurity of a white out. My vision was gone again!

Using the fixed line as a guide, I started across but quickly realized that I had no depth perception due to the white-out conditions. Walking in that white out was like moving through a bright-white, crystallized cloud, which distorted my vision to the point of complete disorientation. The whiteness of the sky blended into the whiteness of the snow making it impossible to distinguish between what was solid and what was not. And on the sheer, snowy slope of the Yellow Band, a step too far to the right would be onto nothing but air. Even clipped onto the rope, a fall from there could be fatal, not only for the person who fell, but also for anyone else on that section of rope, and the white-out conditions dramatically increased that risk. So we went from one anchor to the next, with a single climber on each section of rope. That way if someone fell, the rest of us would have a chance to save ourselves, and if the anchors held, maybe we'd be able to help the fallen climber.

The white out made the air thick with ice particles, which stuck to everything, including the rope and my gloves. I tried to use the arm-wrap to descend the steeper sections, but no matter how tightly I gripped the icy rope, it just slipped through my hands. My descent became a marginally-controlled, rope-slide using leg strength and spiked-feet to slow my speed. It certainly wasn't an eloquent display of climbing technique, but it worked, and section by section I got further down the mountain.

I finally came to the steep wall that led off the Yellow Band. It had only been two days since I'd last climbed it, but during that time, the snow and high winds had transformed it into an almost impenetrable surface of blue-ice glass, on which I now had to rappel down. I stepped onto a tiny platform next to the anchor and kicked my crampon-spikes into the hard ice. I unclipped my figure-eight rappel device from my harness and wrapped the icy rope around it. After checking that it was correctly threaded, I clipped the figure-eight onto a locking-carbineer attached to my harness. I was set up and ready to go, but before starting, I paused and looked down. My heart began to beat faster at the thought of rappelling on an icy rope, wearing icy gloves, on a wall of steely-blue ice, but I wanted down, and this was the only way.

———

Once off the Yellow Band, we started across the traverse that led to where we would continue our descent. It was a relatively short, easy walk that ended at one of the steepest parts of the Lhotse Face. The slope conditions here made using the arm-wrap too dangerous, so we set up to rappel. I was waiting to go down a particularly long, steep section when Bill suddenly descended from above. He said that he was in radio contact with Scott and that everyone was making their way down. Then as quickly as he'd appeared, Bill was gone. I was relieved to hear the news. I had occasionally met up with one of the team at an anchor, but that was about the only time I saw anyone. The combination of the white-out conditions and the terrain had made it impossible to maintain visual contact with the others.

I was about halfway down the steep section when I noticed that the rope below was leading me toward a large crevasse, so I swung to the left and continued down. By the time I was level with the crevasse, I saw that it was actually the platform we'd used for Camp 3. And there sat Bill, along with several of the Sherpas, having a snack. Cool! I climbed over to the rope leading onto the ledge and walked over and sat down next to Bill. Within minutes, Ania, Vivian, and the rest of the team descended onto the platform. Everyone had made it this far, and it was time for a quick break. We had made it back down to 23,500 feet, but we still had more than 2,000 feet to go.

Vivian, Ania, and me taking at break at Camp 3.
(Photo by Bill Allen)

The climb down from Camp 3 was steep but fairly straight forward – arm-wrap here, rappel there. But descending the final section of the Lhotse Face was where it got a bit tricky. There were two ropes leading toward the base, neither one looked like an easy climb. I recalled that coming up this part had been challenging, and expected going down would be too. I just had to go slow and be careful. Once I was down this section, I would be off the Lhotse Face. But I couldn't get ahead of myself; I had to stay focused on the task at hand. I had a hard bit of climbing to finish, it was midday, and the new snow deposited by the storm made this prime avalanche conditions.

———

Once down, I quickly unwrapped my rappel device and hurried away from the base of the Lhotse Face. After walking a relatively safe distance, we stopped, took off our packs, sat down, and stretched out on the snow. We were greeted by two Sherpas, who had come up from Camp 2 with a large thermos of hot lemon tea and bags full of cheese, crackers, olives, and nuts. As we sat enjoying our semi-celebration, I felt relieved that we had all made it safely this far down the mountain. Even though we were still at almost 22,000 feet, we no longer needed the supplemental oxygen, we could relax long enough to eat and drink, and Camp 2 (where we'd spend the night) was an easy 30-minute walk away.

I sat on the snow reclining on my backpack. I was exhausted and not really hungry, but I knew that I had to eat. I pulled off my gloves, reached into the bag, and grabbed a couple of pieces of cheese, and as I ate, I noticed that my fingertips had a slight black tinge to them. At first I thought my eyes were playing tricks on me, so I asked Ania if my fingers looked black. She said that they did. Weird. Was that from my black gloves? Maybe the color had rubbed off. Then I realized how stupid that was. I'd been wearing those gloves for six weeks. Bill and Scott had overheard the conversation and walked over to take a look. They both agreed that it appeared that I may have suffered some minor tissue damage and suggested that I keep using oxygen until I got down to camp. I mentioned that my mask was broken, so Ania let me use hers, and after swapping out the masks, we headed down.

As I walked, I noticed that our camp site had been reduced to the large, white kitchen tent and the orange dining tent. It looked like everything else had already been taken down to Base Camp. The season was ending, we had summited, and it was time to clear off the mountain. And if everything went as planned, we would be back at Base Camp by lunchtime the next day.

———

Ania was the first to walk into Camp 2 with Scott and me close behind. As we approached, Sherpas appeared clanging pots and shouting congratulations. I smiled like the cheshire cat from Lewis Carroll's *Alice's Adventures in Wonderland*. This was the first moment that I had allowed myself to celebrate the fact that I had summited Mt. Everest! Yes, we still had to climb down the Khumbu Icefall one final time and I couldn't truly celebrate until we were all safely back at Base Camp, so I tempered my emotions and tried to stay focused.

I walked over to the tent, dropped my pack on the ground, and reached up to loosen the waist-strap of my climbing harness. The instant my fingers touched the metal buckle, an intense, electrifying bolt of pain shot up my arm! I had felt an uncomfortable tingling sensation in my fingers while I was walking down to Camp 2, but I hadn't thought much of it. Now, that tingling had progressed to pain. The increasing blackness of my fingertips was indicative of tissue damage, but the degree of damage was yet to manifest. For now, I had to protect my fingers by keeping them warm and not using them, but that wasn't going to be easy. Come tomorrow, I was climbing down this mountain with or without the use of my fingers!

———

One by one, everyone piled into the orange tent, unrolled their sleeping pads, and staked out a spot. Just like the slumber parties of youth, tonight we'd sleep head-to-toe snuggled between boots and backpacks. Before we'd gone for the summit, each of us had left behind a small bag of personal items, and all of those stuff-sacks were lined up along one wall of the tent. My bag contained some extra medication, a fresh pair of climbing socks, and a change of clothes. I had lived in my big, bulky down suit for five days straight, and I was more than ready to get out of it and put on my regular climbing clothes. I went to grab my sack, but it wasn't there, so I went out and looked inside the white tent. It wasn't there either. As it turned out, when the Sherpas had packed up the camp and carried some stuff down to Base Camp, they had accidentally taken Ania's and my bags too. That meant no fresh socks and no other clothes for either us of. While I wasn't happy about it, I had a much bigger problem with which to contend.

By now my fingertips felt like they were on fire, and the slightest touch evoked involuntarily outcries of pain. Dang! I could handle pain, but this was so shocking it literally took my breath away! Pain or no pain, I had to get some things done, so I told myself to shut up and deal with it! Using my knuckles, I untied my outer boots and pulled them off, and then I removed my boot-liners. It felt so good to free my feet, never mind the smell. As I grabbed my pack, I yelped from the pain. As hard as I tried not to, I kept brushing my fingertips on things. How could I not? They were attached to my hands. Finally, I got to a point where I just did what I needed to do as I attempted to stifle my cries.

———

Everyone was working on getting their equipment squared away so we could crawl inside our sleeping bags and relax. I had just stuck my cold, stinky feet into my bag, when someone asked me what was wrong with my face. My face?! What about it? I had no idea what they were talking about, but everyone kept insisting that something was wrong with my cheeks. I was tired and distracted by my fingers; I didn't care what my face looked like. So I told them that whatever they saw must have been caused by the sharp edges of the shields on my glacier glasses, and I left it at that. A little while later Scott came in and asked me what was wrong with my face. I really had no idea what everyone was so concerned about. It wasn't like I had a mirror, and I was getting irritated by their continued insistence that something was wrong. Then someone said, "Cindy, your cheeks are swelling up and turning black!" Great!

Happy to be back at Camp 2. (Photo by Vivian Rigney)

Black fingertips and black cheeks, I was starting to think that somehow my vascular disease was causing or exacerbating these injuries. I noticed that other teammates had various ailments, but their skin wasn't turning black. Why was mine? Scott went outside to call the doctors at Base Camp to get their opinions. Both Dr. Hackett and Dr. Steve knew that I had Wegener's Granulomatosis, and I hoped that they could offer some advice. In the meantime, I needed to stay as warm as possible. I was already wearing my down suit but all of my gloves were wet, and there was no way I was putting wet gloves on my blackening fingers.

Paul and Denise came to my rescue. They knew that I didn't have my bag, so they searched through their stuff for an extra pair of gloves, and to my relief, Denise found a soft, dry, light-weight pair. Perfect. I thanked her a thousand times. I was really getting worried about my fingers. It was obvious they were getting worse, not better. I could handle the pain, but the idea of descending the Khumbu Icefall without the use of my fingers was beyond my psychological grasp.

———

Scott came back into the tent and said that I should sleep using oxygen. I was lying next to Paul and he had seen the difficulty I was having doing the most minor tasks, so he once again offered to help. I knew he was tried too and I hated feeling so helpless, but I needed to protect my fingers, so I accepted his offer. Paul got out of his bag and rounded up a few partially-used oxygen bottles. He placed them at the foot of my bag, checked the amount of oxygen in each bottle, and arranged them so that I could use the fullest one when I planned to go to sleep. Then he set up my oxygen system and tucked the bottles between our sleeping pads so I could easily reach them during the night. I was so grateful for his help. Under those conditions, it's difficult to describe how much such simple acts of kindness meant! Paul and Denise, "Thank you from the depths of my heart!"

———

The sun was setting and the temperature was dropping, but Bill still hadn't returned to the tent. We knew that there were several rescues in progress. Earlier that day, a female climber was descending the upper part of the Khumbu Icefall when it collapsed. She had reportedly gone down with tons of ice and had been rescued, but there was only speculation as to her current condition. We were told she was at Camp 1 waiting to be evacuated by the rescue helicopter in the morning, weather permitting.

Bill's absence was later explained; he was assisting another group with a very sick climber, the same climber we'd seen at The Balcony the previous day. In an effort to help the sick climber, Scott had loaned them one of our Sherpas and had given them some of our extra oxygen. I believe the climber was suffering from cerebral edema (swelling of the brain). Fortunately, they managed to get him down to Camp 2, and Bill was helping to stabilize his condition until he could be flown off the mountain.

———

The last thing I remember before allowing myself to succumb to fatigue, was putting on Ania's mask, turning on my oxygen, and checking the flow indicator.

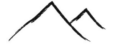

Chapter 17

JUST DEAL WITH IT!

Spasms of pain from my fingers woke me from a coma-like sleep. It was about 2 AM and so dark inside the tent that I couldn't tell if anyone else was awake. I didn't want to make any noise, but I knew my oxygen bottle was empty and I felt suffocated by the mask. I reached up to remove it, but it wouldn't come off. It was stuck to my face! By that point, I didn't think anything could surprise me, but what was going on?!

I removed my gloves and ever so carefully, peeled the mask from my face. I held it trying to figure out why it had stuck to my skin. The mask wasn't frozen, so what was it? My face! Using the backs of my hands I touched my face, and the skin was raw and sticky. Well, that explained it. The ooze from my damaged skin had dried into a crusty adhesive, bonding the mask to my face. It was so bizarre that I had to investigate further. Gently, I cupped my face with the palms of my hands and found that my cheeks were swollen. In fact, my left cheek was so swollen that I couldn't see out of that eye. At least it was my bad eye. Whatever. I was getting off this mountain and one eye would do just fine.

———

With the mask mystery solved, the next thing I had to do was to take my medication. I sat up to get it but I couldn't see a thing, and I didn't want to turn on my headlamp and wake up everyone else. I shifted my focus from my face back to my fingers. While I couldn't see them, my fingers felt stiff and puffy, and the pain was worse. Every time I touched something, thousands of nerves screamed as if I had stuck my fingers into fire! It was shockingly painful, but there was nothing I could do. I had to find and take my medication, and I needed my fingers to that, so I devised a pain-management plan. If I knew I was going to touch something, I anticipated the pain, steeled myself, and locked my jaws to stop my yelps, but the surprise encounters still caught me off guard. I steadied myself and proceeded to search my sleeping bag and backpack for my pills and water. By the time I finished taking my meds, someone had turned on a light. It was time for everyone to get up and get ready – we were going down.

————

I crawled out of my big, down sleeping bag, and using my knuckles, started stuffing it into my backpack. I managed to get it inside, but it had to be compressed so that I had enough space for the rest of my gear. I tried pushing it down, but the pain in my fingers was at an all-time high, and I was becoming increasingly concerned that using my fingers was causing more damage to the already blackened tissue. Bill was next to me packing his own gear. I told him that I couldn't stuff down my sleeping bag because it hurt too much and I asked if he would help. He did. I felt pretty stupid not being able to pack my own gear, but what else could I do?

After I got the rest of my gear into my backpack, I somehow managed to put on my boots, but how on earth was I going to thread my climbing-harness buckle? Embarrassed, I went outside the tent and was trying to put on my harness when Bill came out and saw me. He said, "Cindy! What are you doing out here in the cold? Come in the tent and put it on." I went inside, and using my knuckles, and an occasional fingertip, I finally secured my harness.

———

We started out of camp and headed down to the predetermined point where we would put on our crampons. When we got there, I walked a short distance away from the group before I stopped and took out my crampons. How was I going to do this? The hair on my arms prickled with stubbornness. I was not going to ask for help again. I was becoming increasingly frustrated with my situation, and was determined to work through the pain.

After several minutes I had one crampon on, but I couldn't set the back clip on the other one. Scott walked over and saw me struggling. Shaking his head, he reached down, clipped on my crampon, and scolded me for using my fingers. He was right, and I knew it.

———

I was mad, mad at myself! Over the past three years I had struggled, suffered, and sacrificed so much to make it this far, and now, on the last day of this extreme adventure, I couldn't get over the fact that I was injured and needed help. But the thought of needing assistance was quickly being overshadowed by another, much more daunting matter manifesting in my mind: without the use of my fingers, how was I going to get down the Khumbu Icefall!?!

———

Immersed in a pool of frustration and self-contempt, I headed down through the Western Cwm. After a while, Vivian came up to me and we continued together. As we walked, he told me about various life experiences he'd had and related them to my current situation. Although we'd only met seven weeks ago, Vivian had developed an awareness about me that I don't think could have evolved in any other environment. High on the mountain, there was nowhere to hide, and the extremes of Everest stripped people down to their core beings. Combining this knowledge with his past observations, Vivian, in a sensitive yet direct manner, described what he thought was going on inside my head. He said that I was beating myself up for no reason, that I was a strong person and that I wouldn't have made it this far if I wasn't. Then, he stepped in front of me and continued down the valley. It didn't take long for me to process what he'd said. Vivian was right. I needed to pull up my bootstraps and get myself together. Vivian, "Thank you for that talk!"

———

The sun began to rise as I continued down. With the exception of my talk with Vivian, my descent through the Western Cwm was uneventful. On long, monotonous sections, I often switched into a dreamlike, mechanical state — one step, one jump, one ladder. I knew we were all going to meet at what was left of Camp 1. There, we would take a short break to adjust clothing and equipment before heading down into the Khumbu Icefall.

———

As I approached Camp 1, I heard a distant but distinct sound, and within minutes, the red-and-white helicopter appeared from below. It had come to rescue the crippled climbers: the woman who had been caught in the icefall collapse, and the man who was very ill with cerebral edema. I'd been so lost in my own comparatively minor concerns that I had forgotten that there were people on Everest fighting for their lives, and the thunderous sound of the helicopter's rotors brought me crashing back into reality.

———

Part of the team was already at Camp 1 when I walked up. Instinctively, I took off my pack and pulled out my water bottle. Then it hit me! Because my change of clothes had inadvertently been sent down the mountain, I was going to have to descend the Khumbu Icefall in my bulky, HOT down suit. I was roasting just standing there, but once I started to climb, I would surely overheat! And I'd already experienced the dangerous effects of heat exhaustion on the way up when I wasn't wearing a down suit!

At first I just complained about not having my other climbing clothes, but the more I talked, the more upset I got. I'd already come to terms with the fact that I was going to have to descend without the use of my fingertips, but now the full reality of the situation hit home. Within minutes, I would be on an extremely dangerous section of the mountain, which had collapsed the day before, in my down suit! Immediately someone, I think it was Denise, offered me a pair of pants, but Ania had just walked up and she didn't have her clothes either. I declined the pants and said that Ania needed them. I'm not going to lie and say I did it for any identifiable reason. All I can say is that I was mad and refused the pants out of anger at my situation. Then Paul offered me his down pants, but again I refused, saying they'd be too big. And anyway, to change clothes meant that I'd have to remove all of my gear: my harness, my crampons, my boots – everything! And if I had trouble doing it back at camp, how was I going to do it here!?!

Everyone was offering suggestions but I'd had enough, and I snapped! I threw up my arms, told everyone to be quiet, and I turned my back to the group. Now, I know myself and knew that I just needed to voice my frustration and then would immediately regain my composure. I just needed a minute. Sure enough, I calmed down, turned back to the group, and apologized to everyone. I'd had a monumental meltdown, and I was so embarrassed; embarrassed by my behavior, and embarrassed by the fact that in order to change clothes I would have to ask my teammates to help me put my gear back on – again! Still inwardly seething, I accepted Paul's pants and Bill's down sweater, and with the help of several teammates, I changed out of my down suit.

———

It was such a stupid moment, my little breakdown. It was pride that had gotten in my way, and thank goodness it had only lasted for a few minutes because "pride" has claimed many lives on this mountain.

———

As we made our way down from Camp 1, I noticed that the glacial-valley was more "valley" than "glacier." What had been here on the way up, was now gone. The glacier was disappearing right out from under our feet. The ladders were very unstable and the crevasses we had to jump were much wider. At first I didn't realize the extent of the change, but as we got closer to the icefall, the landscape became stunning – literally!

While standing on an ice-bridge waiting for my turn to cross a crevasse, I looked to my left across the valley toward Mt. Nuptse. When we had come up, just six days earlier, it had been mostly solid. Now the entire center was gone, and what remained, resembled a giant, white hand with long, twisted fingers of ice. I was shocked to see how quickly and severely the glacier had changed, and I knew that more change could happen at any moment and any place, including right where I was standing!

Scott was leading with Ania, and I was close behind. After crossing some particularly precarious places, we reached the top edge of the icefall, which was considerably narrower now. On the first two rotations we had rappelled down the 70-foot ice wall, but there had been a collapse near here the day before, so Scott told us to stay put while he went over to make sure the anchors and ropes were still in place and secure. The tension in the air was palpable. Finally, he signaled Ania to come over. From a distance, I watched as she set up her rappelling equipment and started down. Then Scott waved to me. I walked over and stepped onto a small, one-foot square platform to set up for my rappel. I know I used my fingertips to get down, but I don't remember feeling any pain. Motivation is a powerful instrument.

There were two ropes. Ania was on one and I went down the other. She landed on a narrow ledge, clipped onto the rope, and started across with me right behind her. The ledge was only wide enough for a single boot so we walked placing one foot in front of the other. To my left was the towering ice-wall and to my right was nothing but air. Falling here was not an option, but that wasn't my biggest concern. A collapse had occurred in this area the day before, taking down a female climber in tons of ice debris. Ania quickly but carefully walked along the ledge until she came to a large crevasse. I pulled up right behind her and stared – where was the ladder?

Just then, Scott came up from behind and said that we were going to have to jump. It was a huge crevasse, larger than any we'd jumped before, and we had full packs on our backs. But there was no choice. We had to get out of this area and seconds mattered! Ania stepped up to the very lip of the edge; she had to get as close as possible in order to shorten the jumping distance. Then, like a cat, she sprung across the crevasse and landed with all four claws dug in. She paused for a few seconds and then scrambled up the side. She had made it! Now, it was my turn!

After almost two months on the mountain, climbing to the summit, and already crossing the icefall five times, this was my first moment of uncertainty. In the past, no matter what the challenge, I would shift into my *10-feet-at-a-time* mode, and just do it. But not this time; this was different. I'm not sure why it was different, but I can remember clear as day, my exact thoughts and feelings during that moment, and let me tell you, "feelings" on Everest were not good.

I walked up to the slanted edge of the lip. Fighting the instinct to look down, I focused on the far side. I needed to jump, but first I had to figure out how I was going to project myself so that I landed on the ice and not in the crevasse. I inched closer, dug my crampon-tips into the ice, and leaned slightly over the lip. I didn't look down. If I fell I would find out what was down there. I tried to focus on getting across, as these thoughts flickered through my mind, "If Larry knew what I was going to do, he'd kill me. I'm going to die! Stop that!" Then I jumped.

I landed with both hands and both feet dug into the ice, and without taking a breath, I froze in place. Once I realized that I was safe, I quickly scrambled up the slope and onto an ice bridge. Then I climbed down a ladder onto a narrow ice pinnacle that led to a double ladder. Once up that double ladder, I followed the slope to another large crevasse with another double ladder perched precariously across it. Ania had already clipped on and was stepping onto the ladder when it suddenly twisted about 30 degrees to her left. Instinctively, she used her body weight to counter the movement, righted herself, and continued across.

I felt the ice move under my feet as I stood waiting. I knew that a collapse could occur within a blink-of-an-eye and the thought was quite alarming! But this was no place for such thoughts or feelings. They had to be stored away, out of reach, to be dealt with later. What mattered now was getting across that ladder, and it was going to be tricky. The ice had melted to the point that the ladder was barely touching the edge on one side, and hanging in the air suspended by several anchored ropes on the other. I watched as Ania finished crossing. It was now my turn. I stepped up to clip on, but to which rope? There were so many. I took a breath, looked closer, found the correct rope, clipped on, turned around, and stepped onto the ladder. It twisted, I adjusted, and before I knew it, I was across and headed for the next series of ice bridges and ladders.

———

Time passed and we continued down through an amalgamation of crevasses, ladders, ice walls, clipping and unclipping. Fueled by adrenaline and climbing on instinct, my only thought was of getting off the crumbling icefall. I finally got to a place where, in the far distance, I could see the multicolored tents of Base Camp. It was still hours away, but only hours! Not long after that, we came down a steep section, rounded a corner, and walked onto the first relatively-safe, flat area since leaving Camp 1. Three other climbers were sitting there taking a break and we joined them. It was the first time in days that I felt a sense of relief, of safety. We were still in the icefall, and not quite out of danger, but we were getting there.

The rest of the team soon joined us, and it only took a second for the backpacks to come off and the cameras to come out. Someone asked one of the other climbers to take our picture, so we handed him all of our cameras and gathered for the photos. Paul and Denise were on the left, I was in the back, and Vivian, Bill, and Scott were sitting on their packs in front of us. And right before the picture was snapped, Ania flung herself across their laps landing with her head resting on her arm and a big smile on her white, sun-screened face.

Our smiles say it all! (Photo courtesy of Ania Lichota)

After a well-earned break, we headed down the final section of the Khumbu Icefall. I could see our camp and knew that we were only about 45 minutes away! As we continued descending, I noticed that Scott had been making a lot of radio calls. I assumed he was checking on our Sherpas, who were on their way down with the remainder of the Camp 2 equipment. We were traversing through a twisty, hilly section when I heard shouting, not frantic shouts like something was wrong, just shouting. I rounded a corner, and saw a group of people gathered on a small plateau. They were looking down at me and yelling. I couldn't understand what they were saying, but as I got closer I could tell that they weren't climbers. It was Dawa, our head Sherpa, and some of our Base Camp Sherpas! That's what Scott had been up to. He'd been radioing our progress to Base Camp so that the Sherpas could set up a celebration for us. I climbed onto the plateau to the cadence of cheering congratulations.

Once at the top, I gave each Sherpa a big hug, and then turned and hugged everyone on our team. None of us could stop smiling and laughing! We had summited Mt. Everest and everyone had made it safely back down! The celebration could begin!

There were cookies, candy, crackers, and cheese, and each of us was handed a bottle of Fanta or Coca-Cola. And proudly planted in the snow was a beautifully hand-painted sign made by the Sherpas that read, "Mountain Trip Team, Hearty Congratulation Successful Summit, Everest Expedition 2010-5-23" with three pretty, pink flowers painted along the bottom.

I could finally relax. After I ate some cookies and drank my Fanta, I asked Ania if she would take a picture of me sitting in front of our beautiful summit sign, and it's one of my favorite photos from the entire adventure! The picture shows what words can never express: the joy in my smile and the enchantment in my eyes, a portal into my very heart and soul!

Success! (Photo by Ania Lichota)

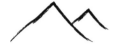

Chapter 18

UNBELIEVABLE RELIEF

It was late morning on May 25th when I stepped out of the Khumbu Icefall for the last time – mission accomplished! Slowly I walked toward our Base Camp. There was no longer any need to hurry, no ladders to cross, no crevasses to jump, no seracs to fall and bury me. I was finally free of all those dangers, and for the first time, in what seemed to be forever, I felt safe!

In the distance, I heard clanging pots and shouts of welcome and congratulations. I crossed the small river and was heading toward my tent when I heard music, and not just any music. Michael Jackson's "Thriller" was thundering through camp. The Sherpas were blasting our "welcome home" song, and it was a perfect choice! The rhythm pulsated through the air and into my exhausted limbs. Smiling, I swung my arms to the beat of the music, and in my big boots and crampons, I danced across the rocks, up the small hill, and into my tent. I quickly stripped off my gear, changed my socks and boots, and headed toward the dining tent, hugging every Sherpa I passed along the way.

After a few minutes of hugs and handshakes, I put my thoughts of celebration on hold. I had a couple of things to do. I needed to get over to the Everest ER and see Dr. Steve about my eyes, face, and fingers, and I needed to wash-up. I hadn't bathed in a week and I wanted to be clean in case the doctor put medicine in my eyes or on my face. I walked over to Dawa Sherpa and asked him if I could get a bucket of water. I told him that it didn't matter if the water was hot or cold, I just needed to wash before seeing the doctor. He nodded and hand-ed me a bucket of warm water. Before leaving, I went into the dining tent to tell Scott I was going over to see Dr. Steve and not to hold lunch for me. Ania was inside, sitting at the table, and she said that she'd go with me.

The walk from our camp to the Everest ER took about 15 minutes, and I usually had no trouble locating it, but Base Camp had changed quite a lot while we were up on the moun-tain. It was spring, the ice was melting, the river was rushing, and many of the tents had been packed-up for the season. Some of the basic landmarks were still in place. The most dis-tinctive one was a boulder the size of a car that was precari-ously perched on top of a pointed pinnacle of ice. I couldn't be-lieve that it hadn't fallen yet. The ice holding it up was almost melted and it was just a matter of time before it would come crashing down, destroying everything in its path. We swung wide to the left and headed up the trail that ended at the ER.

As we walked up to the big, white medical tent, we could hear that Dr. Steve was busy inside with someone else, so we sat on the ground and waited. After 10 minutes or so, a man came out followed by Dr. Steve. When he saw us waiting, he smiled and invited us to join him for some tea in his dining tent. After several minutes of general conversation, Dr. Steve asked us about our injuries. Ania and Dr. Steve discussed her injuries and prognosis, and then he turned to me. First Dr. Steve looked at my eyes and told me that I had a bit of snow blindness, but it wasn't bad. Then he checked my swollen, black cheeks and fingertips. He said that I had "cold damage" but not "frostbite," and explained the difference. The tissues of my cheeks and fin-gertips had been damaged by cold-exposure, but they had not frozen solid (frostbite). While cold-damaged flesh dies along with the nerves, both grow back in about 3 months. This was great news! I'd be returning home with numb, but whole fingers!

It was good news all around, and with minor treatment, our injuries would heal. As we walked over to the medical tent, I asked Dr. Steve what he was going to do with his baseball hat adorned with the large, white flower. He said that he hadn't thought about it, but that he'd probably hang it on his wall at home as a reminder of this Everest season's events. He also told us that the Everest ER was closing, and he'd be leaving the next day. After getting our medications, Ania and I hugged Dr. Steve and said our farewells.

———

I walked back to our camp overcome with relief. My injuries were from cold-exposure and not a consequence of the Wegener's. I had climbed to the top of the world and held the NORD banner, a symbol of hope for so many people whose lives are significantly affected by rare diseases or disorders. Why was I, one of those people, able to do it? A question that still remains unanswered.

———

After lunch I sent an e-mail to my family and told them that I was safe, in good health (relative to having just summited Everest), and would be leaving Base Camp the day after next. Since there was no reason to immediately start packing, I spent the afternoon resting in my tent. After waking from a nap, I took my pills, and headed for our dining tent. Some of the team was already there and the others soon followed, signaling the beginning of a seemingly endless procession of food. Sherpas paraded into the tent carrying shining, silver platters of meats, cheeses, popcorn, pizza, fresh fruits and vegetables, chicken, fish, freshly baked croissants, and a large tureen containing a wonderful potato soup. Serki had truly outdone himself with this unbelievable feast!

We were all sitting around the table after dinner when several Sherpas entered the tent and proudly presented us with a beautifully decorated "Summit Cake!" At almost 18,000 feet, Serki had worked his magic – again! I was so exhausted that I could hardly move, but I forced myself to get up and walk to the other side of the table to take a picture. It was a good thing that I moved because within minutes the dining tent was packed with people. Everyone toasted and cheered as Scott cut the cake, and then one of the Sherpas went over to the communications table and put on "Thriller." The effect was akin to setting a spark to kindling – it ignited a celebration! We all circled the table, dancing and singing and laughing. I have no idea how I was even able to stand, let alone dance, but my exhaustion evaporated into an energy that radiated from deep within, and we danced into the night.

Cheers!

———

Before breakfast the next morning, I went down to the dining tent and got the satellite phone. I had a post-summit, radio interview scheduled, but first I wanted to talk with Larry. I called but he wasn't home. So I called Rob Strauss, Associate Producer for *All Things Considered*, which airs on Southern California Public Radio. Amazingly, the call went through on the first try and Rob connected me with host, Alex Cohen. At one point during the interview Alex said, "It sounds like you don't believe you did it." She was correct; I didn't.

———

I had climbed through the dangerous Khumbu Icefall six times, stood on the top of the world, and was now safely back at Base Camp, but the experience had left me feeling as if I were one of the mummies from the Michael Jackson "Thriller" video. I moved slowly and purposefully, and I felt empty and numb. For years I had imagined what this day, this moment, would feel like, and this wasn't it! In hindsight, I believe that until a person has been through this kind of extreme experience, there is no way to even begin to understand what it's going to be like. I couldn't, and I had just done it! I knew what I had accomplished, yet my brain couldn't fully comprehend it. It was too soon and too much to absorb. I was back in the same tent that I had lived in for almost six weeks, but everything seemed different. I was different. I was living in a kind of detached awareness. I was cognizant of my surroundings, yet apathetic and unfeeling, with one exception – an overwhelming need to get home to my family!

———

After breakfast, it was time to start packing. We were leaving Base Camp the next morning. Scott and Bill worked on disassembling and storing all of the electronics and we tried to help by organizing the remaining foods items. The Sherpas, however, were the professionals, and in the end, it was best to just stay out of their way. As the hours passed, I watched our camp disappear into a dozen large, blue barrels that yaks would carry down to Lukla. It was finally time for me to pack, so I headed up to my tent.

Everything was already stored in my two big, green duffle bags, but I had to separate the gear I was taking down in my backpack from the gear that would go down with the yaks. Thankfully, the nerves in my fingertips were already dying, lessening the pain, which made packing much easier. As I went through my things, I picked out some items that I knew our Sherpas could use: a sleeping bag and pad, my crampons, some clothing, a knife, water bottles, a first-aid kit, a bag of extra batteries, and a hiking pole – the mate of the one that had become part of the Western Cwm. I packed it all into a bag, took it down to Dawa, and asked him to distribute the things as he thought best. Then I walked into the dining tent, sat down, and wrote the final entry in my Mt. Everest journal:

> ### May 26th
>
> *We did it! Summited on May 23rd at 9:02 AM. Camp 4 to Camp 4 took 18.5 hours! Over 150 climbers! Very, very hard. No sane person should do this! But I did ☺ Some nerve damage in fingers and cheeks but Dr. Steve said will repair. Just called **NPR** and trying to get Larry. Want early flight out!*

Fifty-six days earlier I had walked away from my home and my family, and embarked on an adventure of a lifetime. From the moment that I stepped across the thick black line on the airport floor, it had felt like I had been living in some kind of dream world. Once my goal was accomplished, I was obsessed with a single thought – get back to "my" world as quickly as possible!

Later that day I made my last blog post from Base Camp:

Said Goodbye to Mt. Everest Base Camp!

We are making our way back to civilization: a bed, shower, toilets, etc... With luck, we will be in Kathmandu tomorrow – I HOPE!!!!

Thank you so much for all of your comments. They mean a great deal to me. Climbing Mt. Everest was the most difficult thing I have ever done! I will tell you that at no point did I think to stop and turn around! However, by the time I reached the summit I was in a state of amazement at the physical, mental, and emotional feat I had just accomplished – to stand (or sit as in the picture) and look down at the rest of the world. I reached beyond the clouds and I touched it!

Now, all I want is to get home to my family.

I will post a full story when I have recovered for a few days. Right now I have numb fingertips and a cold-scarred face.

The Khumbu Icefall was becoming more dangerous with each passing day. Once all the climbers and Sherpas were down, the Icefall Doctors would go up and remove the remaining ladders. By the time we left the mountain, the south side of Everest would be closed for the season.

———

Early the next morning, Dawa escorted Vivian, Ania, and me down to the rocky, Base Camp helicopter landing pad. We were scheduled to take a helicopter down to Lukla, and from there, catch a flight to Kathmandu, which would put us back at the Yak and Yeti Hotel that same day! We stood off to one side watching as the helicopter arrived. As soon as it touched down, several men ran up, opened the side door, reached in, and brought out a body wrapped in thick, orange plastic. Dawa told us that it was the body of the climber we had seen up at Camp 2, and that he had been brought down to be buried. The men set the body on the ground and ushered us in, closing the door behind us. And in the blink of an eye, we were off. It was a well-orchestrated routine: get the helicopter in and out of Base Camp as quickly as possible. Even with the pilot breathing supplemental oxygen, it wasn't safe for him to stay at that altitude, much less the higher altitude from where he'd just come.

It had taken us nine days to trek into Base Camp, but the flight out would only take about 30 minutes! So I relaxed, sat back, and enjoyed the view. It was now springtime and the Khumbu region was bursting with color. As we flew down through the valleys, I was captivated by the contrasting scenery: the bright, green valleys surrounded by the snow-capped giants of the Himalayas. It was hard to believe that just days ago, I stood at the top of the world and looked down on the same mountains at which I was now looking up! Before I knew it, we were landing at the Lukla Airport.

Our flight to Kathmandu wasn't due in for a while so we went to a café to wait. The rest of the team arrived within the hour and we all walked over to the airport and checked in. All I could think about was getting back to Kathmandu.

Once there, I could start working toward getting an earlier flight home. I needed to be home with my family, and my scheduled flight didn't leave until June 4th, which was seven days away!

We watched as the first flight left. We were booked on the next one and I was so excited that I could barely stand it! I was getting closer to home by the hour! We had been waiting about 20 minutes when an airport official came over to our group and told us that our flight was delayed, but because we had already cleared security, we needed to stay in the boarding area. Several hours later, the airport official came back and announced that, due to bad weather, the rest of the day's flights had been cancelled, and that we should check back the following day. No way was this happening!

I walked out of the airport and up the rocky, dirt path leading back to the café. At first, I was in a shock-induced state of numbness, but slowly reality started seeping into my head. By the time I sat down in the plastic chair, I was immersed in a pool of intensely negative emotions, struggling to keep my head up and my thoughts clear. I knew this could happen. In fact, it was quite common, but I hadn't mentally prepared myself for this delay – a major error on my part! As the minutes ticked by, I realized I was losing the composure battle. I just couldn't process the fact that I had to spend one more night on the mountain, in a plywood-walled cube, sleeping on a wooden plank with only the clothes on my back and someone else's dirty blanket! Even worse, I couldn't check to see about getting an earlier flight home! Then my brain tilted, and I got extremely angry! After everything I had been through to climb Everest, this was the first time I thought I might actually lose control – I needed off this mountain!

———

It took most of the afternoon to calm down and when I finally regained my self-control, I was stunned and embarrassed by my own reaction. For goodness sakes, I had just climbed to the top of the world, and on the scale of things that could have gone wrong, getting stuck for one night in Lukla was infinitesimal! For the past two and a half years, I had conquered every obstacle, both the expected and unexpected, by taking things *10-feet-at-a-time*, but between the overwhelming experience of summiting Everest and my extreme mental and physical exhaustion, I had dropped my guard and let my emotions get the best of me.

———

Thankfully, I had lots of minutes left on my satellite SIM card, so later that afternoon I got the satellite phone and started making calls. It was the middle of the night back home, and I didn't want to wake up Larry, so I called Dragon Air to see if I could arrange for an earlier flight from Kathmandu to Hong Kong. They had a seat on a flight that left in three days, but booking it was risky. I could still be trapped in Lukla, and even if I made it to Kathmandu, there was no guarantee that I could get a flight from Hong Kong to Los Angeles. But if I didn't reserve this flight, I wouldn't be able to get home for another week, so I booked it. My thinking was that if I missed the flight, I would be stuck in Kathmandu, and if I made the flight but couldn't get a connection to Los Angeles, I would be stuck in Hong Kong. At this point, I was willing to try anything to get home sooner.

Before going to bed, I talked with Larry and told him where I was and what I was planning. It was so good to hear his voice. Knowing that Teshia was still asleep, I sent her a text message. After I got off the phone, I curled up and went to sleep.

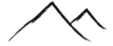

Chapter 19

THERE IS NO PLACE LIKE HOME

In the morning our agent was the first one at the airport and got us scheduled on the first flight out of Lukla, but just like the previous day, there were no guarantees that we'd get out. When we arrived, the airport was full of people trying to book flights. We, however, held boarding passes with the word "one" printed on them, and IF a flight left, we'd be the first ones on it. I stood at the window waiting and watching for a plane to come in from Kathmandu, and then one finally did! Everyone immediately started moving toward the doorway. It was so jammed with bodies that I had to wriggle my way through while flashing my boarding pass. I finally got out the door and walked over to the plane, but I knew not to count my chickens before they hatched, and I didn't relax until we were off the runway and in the air.

As I sat waiting in my seat, people started talking about the upcoming takeoff. Lukla's airport had justly earned the title of *World's Most Dangerous Airport*. Its runway was extremely short and narrow (1,500 feet by 65 feet) with a 12% slope, and it was bordered on one end by a mountain-side, and on the other, by a 2,000-foot sheer drop-off. It didn't faze me though, I just wanted out of there! Finally, the pilots boarded the small plane and started the engine. So far so good! They taxied out onto the short strip of black asphalt and revved up the engine for takeoff. The roar was deafening and the plane shook as it fought against its own power.

Then the pilot released the brake and the plane sped down the runway, and just as the asphalt disappeared, we lifted into the air.

———

We arrived at the Yak and Yeti Hotel later that morning. Fantastic! We were in Kathmandu, and our gear was on its way to Lukla via yaks. With luck, it would arrive in a day or two. I, however, was back in civilization and there wasn't anything that I needed in those bags! My backpack contained most of my personal stuff: my journal, cameras, and extra medications. And before we had left to climb Everest, we'd each checked a bag into the hotel's storage room. Those bags contained our "city stuff." We checked in at the front desk, retrieved our stored bags, and proceeded to our rooms.

The most basic things became extravagant luxuries after living for so long on the mountain. I walked into my room and opened the windows. A warm breeze caressed my face as I stood admiring the beautiful green gardens. I placed my small "city" bag on the bed, and opened it as if it was a gift of great value, and it was. Inside were my personal belongings including some clean clothes! But first things first, I grabbed my soap and shampoo and headed for the shower. I reached behind the curtain and turned on the hot water, and it was hot! I stood in the shower for the longest time reveling in the hot, fresh water. I finally turned it off, and as I stepped out, I glanced at the mirror and froze, shocked by what I saw. I hadn't seen myself for over seven weeks, and what I saw was a skeleton with skin hanging from it! I knew that I'd lost a great deal of weight, but to actually see it was ... well, disturbing. After drying off with the clean, fluffy white towel, I searched through my bag for something to wear. But I had lost so much weight that everything I put on just fell off of my hips. I finally found one pair of shorts that stayed on, and that was good enough. Time to eat.

The hotel's main restaurant was an all-you-can-eat buffet. Just what the doctor ordered. I could pick and choose what I wanted to eat, and I could eat as much as I wanted. Several members of the group were already seated so I joined them. As we sat at the table eating, I laughed and said, "I can't believe a hotel frequented by climbers would offer an all-you-can-eat buffet." One side of the buffet table was lined with a selection of soups, a variety of potato and rice dishes, platters full of curried and roasted chicken, baked and sautéed fish, and several different types of beef and pork items. The other side was covered with trays of fresh fruits and vegetables, breads and cheeses, and a fantastic dessert selection. I think everyone, including me, made at least seven trips to that buffet. I just kept eating and eating, but I never felt full. I only stopped because I didn't want to make myself sick.

———

We were all going into town for a celebratory dinner later that night, but until then we were free to do as we pleased. Over the past six weeks, we had worked as a unit, a team, but now we were once again individuals. Before disbanding to our own devices, Scott gave us a rundown of some of the upcoming events, which included a meeting with Billie Bierling, who was tasked with collecting the statistical information from the Everest 2010 summiters. I said, "Okay, I'll see you all then," and happy as a bird freed from its cage, I flew up to my room and plugged in my netbook.

The hotel was equipped with wireless Internet, so I could sit in the privacy of my room to send and receive e-mails, and post to my blog. It was so wonderful to be able to communicate with my family, friends, and supporters again.

My blog post from May 28th:

Back in Kathmandu!

"WOW is it great to be back in a city! You have no idea what it is to live at 17,500 ft for six weeks in a tent. I am working on an event outline but it will be delayed because we just found out that there is a parade in the morning, we get a medal in the afternoon, and then there is a summiteers' party in the evening! Now is a good time to say that without our wonderful Sherpa team, none of this would have been possible!"

———

A few hours later, we all met in the hotel's foyer and walked through the noisy, city streets to a wonderful outdoor restaurant. The food was fantastic, the ambiance delightful, and everyone had a great time. After dinner we walked across the street and got ice cream for dessert. As much as I enjoyed the evening, my thoughts kept drifting to home. So I said my good nights and headed back to the hotel with the hope that there was an e-mail from Larry or Teshia.

———

My last blog post from Kathmandu.

Busy Day in Kathmandu

"So, yesterday I got up early went to the parade, in the afternoon we received our medals, and then went to the dinner party in the evening.

Our bags are in Lukla. Now let's see if they make it to Kathmandu today. That would be amazing because I could fly home TONIGHT!!!!! Otherwise I have to wait three more days to leave.

I will post the details of the climb with pictures as soon as I can, but my main focus is getting home to my family! I have been gone for two months."

The 3rd Annual International Sagarmatha (Mt. Everest) Day Parade.

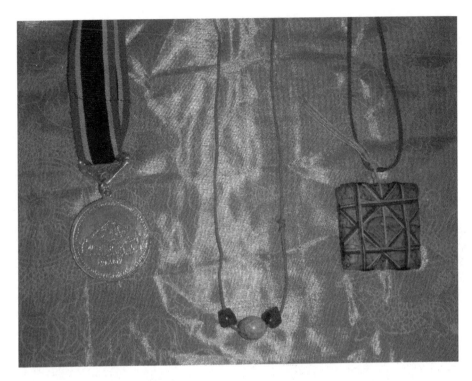

Summiter's Medal from the Nepalese Ministry of Tourism, Blessing Necklace with Dzi stone bead, and Puja Blessing Necklace.

———

Our bags didn't make it in from Lukla and I was booked on a Dragon Air flight that left for Hong Kong that night at midnight. If I cancelled, there wasn't another flight for three days, but if I left as planned, how would I get my bags? Another dilemma, I still didn't have a connecting flight out of Hong Kong. I went to the hotel's concierge desk and asked if there was a way that I could have my bags shipped home. The concierge told me to go to the FedEx office in town and check. Within 10 minutes I was standing in the FedEx office completing the forms to have my bags picked up at the Yak and Yeti Hotel, whenever they arrived from Lukla, and shipped to my home. The cost of shipping the bags was almost the same as spending three more days in Kathmandu when you factored in food and lodging, so the price was a nonissue. I still had to work out two other details though. First, I needed to enlist the help of someone in the group to call FedEx and handle the pick-up when my bags arrived, and second, I needed to get booked on a flight from Hong Kong to Los Angeles. I was, however, willing to get stuck in Hong Kong and work on that issue from there.

I got back to the hotel and told Bill what I was planning. Bill said that he had to stay and wait for the bags, so he'd call FedEx and get my bags picked up. Great, shipping handled! Now my focus shifted to getting a flight out of Kong Hong. Luckily, I still had time left on my SIM card and I asked Bill if I could use one of the satellite phones. He handed me the phone and I took it outside to the hotel's garden to try to find a spot where I could get a connection. The surrounding buildings interfered with the satellite signal, but I finally found a place where it worked. However, if I moved more than a foot in any direction, it disconnected.

While standing on a stone halfway up the garden steps, I got out all of my travel documents, put on my glasses and my headlamp (it was getting dark), and called American Airlines. I had used frequent flier miles for my plane ticket, so getting a seat was going to be tricky. I got through after a few dropped calls, but I had to wait in a queue to get connected with an agent. At first I wasn't overly concerned about running out of SIM time, but after waiting for 20 minutes, I started to worry. I eventually got through to a wonderful woman, who after hearing my situation, was more than willing to help. She found one seat on a flight out of Hong Kong with only a 12-hour layover, but the seat was in First Class. Yikes! I asked her if I had enough miles to upgrade to that seat. She said that I did, so I took it! I couldn't believe it had worked out! I stood there shaking, not from the cool air, but from the realization that I would actually be home in two days!

The agent placed me on hold while she worked on the changes. I was standing there as still as a statue for fear of losing the connection when I heard the phone start to beep. I was running out of time! No way, I had to get this flight! Then I heard her voice. She said that there was a problem with my booking, but that she could fix it. I told her that I was almost out of minutes and the phone was going to disconnect any second. She said, "Don't worry. You're booked on the flight." And the phone went dead.

I anxiously gathered up my stuff and walked back inside to the hotel's Business Center. I logged onto my e-mail, and there it was – my flight confirmation. I printed the precious piece of paper and tucked it into my bag. Then I sent Larry and Teshia an e-mail saying that I was coming home!

———

It had worked, I couldn't believe it! In less than seven hours I would be on my way home! I ran upstairs to pack. On the way to my room I knocked on Bill's door. He answered and I handed him the satellite phone and shared my news. Then I gave him the FedEx paperwork and the money to pay for the shipping. I walked away saying, "Thank you, thank you, thank you!" I was so grateful for Bill's help.

———

I was floating on clouds, barely able to focus on anything but going home. We'd all been invited to dinner, courtesy of one of Scott and Bill's business associates, and I decided to join them although I'd have to leave early due to my 8:30 PM flight check-in time. At dinner I ate but I wasn't hungry, and for one of the first times on the entire trip, I was quiet. I tried to enjoy the final moments with my teammates, but I just kept looking at my watch. The time finally came for me to leave, and since I was the first of the Mountain Trip Mt. Everest 2010 Summit Team to go, it was a bittersweet moment. I stood up and circled the table giving everyone hugs and wishing them safe travel. Then I walked out the door and headed to the airport.

———

I arrived at the Hong Kong Airport and went to the First Class lounge to wait. And I must say that having access to the facilities in the lounge made the 12-hour layover much more pleasant. I love those frequent flier miles. Everything was free: Internet, wonderful food and drinks, and even private cabanas. The cabana featured a full-size bathroom with a large bathtub, and it had its own private patio with lounge chairs and a stream running through it. I took a bath, and then went out and had lunch. I had three more left hours until my flight departed for Los Angeles and home.

I posted this to my blog during my 12-hour layover:

Coming Home!

I will be home by Monday afternoon!!!!!!!!!!!!!! After being away for two months, I cannot describe what it is like to know that in 17 hours I will be home.

It was finally time to board the plane. I strapped on my backpack, grabbed my small bag, and walked to the gate. The final leg of an incredible, once-in-a-lifetime adventure was about to begin.

The flight back to Los Angeles was like a daydream. There I sat in First Class, the lap of luxury, with great food and a glass of wine (or two). I tried to watch a movie, but I couldn't concentrate. I was too excited. So I took out my computer and looked at my pictures, but I still couldn't comprehend what I had done. Against all odds, I had summited Mt. Everest and held the NORD banner on the top of the world. It truly was unbelievable.

———

After being away for exactly 60 days, I walked out of the airport security area and into the arms of my family – I was home.

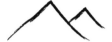

EPILOGUE

Within a week of returning home, I visited both Dr. Gorn and Dr. Kreiger, and to their absolute amazement they found no Wegener's-related adverse effects from my Everest experience. I was, however, both physically and emotionally exhausted. It took almost a month before I felt like myself again.

———

People ask me if I would do it again and I answer that in a way, I already have. To write this book I had to climb Mt. Everest a second time, not with my body, but with my mind, heart, and soul.

During my time on Everest, and especially when climbing, I focused only on the task at hand and sequestered the physical and emotional reality of the moment. I did not allow myself to acknowledge these things. I had, in fact, placed them in such a deep recess of my mind that it was difficult to bring them forth. In order to write this book, I had to take myself back to the mountain and relive not only the actual events, but also the thoughts and feelings I had suppressed. As I remembered and typed the words, I smiled, I cringed, and I cried.

For Rare Disease Day 2011, I made a water-proof NORD banner and took it with me on a diving vacation to Roatan.

From the Top of the World to the Depths of the Sea.

———

People began speculating and asking what I was going to do for the next year's Rare Disease Day, and honestly, I had no idea. There were all kinds of suggestions from swimming to Catalina Island to cycling across America, and then a friend on a Wegener's support blog suggested that I train to run the 1000-mile Alaskan Iditarod Sled Dog Race. I knew a little bit about the Iditarod from an Environmental Exercise Physiology course I took at CSUF but, as with the other suggestions,

I immediately dismissed the idea. I may have summited Mt. Everest but run the Iditarod - that was simply ridiculous. I didn't even snow ski, and I hate being cold!

It was not by coincidence that my friend had mentioned the race. It had, in fact, started a few days earlier. So, out of curiosity, I looked at the Iditarod's website, and that set the tide in motion. Was it ridiculous?

———

In my wildest imagination, I did not think anything could be more difficult than summiting Everest, but I was about to find out that I was wrong.

———

Quandary: how to chronicle the next chapter of my journey? A sequel to this book? No way. My background is technical writing. This book was extremely difficult to write and I vowed never to write another. Solution: capture it on film. Knowing absolutely nothing about film production, I did some research, pulled more money from our retirement account, and hired a small, Alaskan film crew.

———

In the summer of 2011, at the age of 53 and with no previous experience, I went to Alaska and began training under the guidance of Lance Mackey (4-time Iditarod champion and cancer survivor) at his Comeback Kennel. I immediately fell in love with the sport, the Alaskan people and culture, but most of all, I fell in love with the world's most amazing athletes - the dogs!

Me hugging Baby Drool and Raven waiting his turn.

I spent the next two years flying back and forth between California and Alaska in order to train and run the required races. This sport takes a tremendous amount of work and dedication, not to mention dealing with the extremes of Alaskan winters with temperatures regularly 20-60 degrees below zero and as little as 4 hours of light per day. I would typically step off the plane into a 110-degree temperature difference, get to the kennel, walk to my shed, change my clothes, go out to the yard, hook-up my team, and head out into the darkness with the dogs. I was determined, and on January 28, 2013, I completed my final qualifying race. The next morning, just days before the deadline, I submitted my application to the Iditarod Trail Committee (ITC). A few days later, I was notified that I had been approved by the ITC qualifying board and I became the 69th and final musher to enter the 2013 Iditarod, The Last Great Race on Earth.

My racing motto is VASCULITIS: Racing for Life.

*Coming in at the end of the Iditarod Ceremonial Run,
March 2, 2013.*

On March 3, 2013, my team of amazing canine athletes
and I left the Iditarod start-line and headed out for the 1000-
mile run across the Alaskan wilderness. A few weeks before
the race, I'd injured my leg, but I didn't go see a doctor. I
thought it was just a pulled muscle; and at this point, what
was a little pain.

About 20 miles out from the start, I reinjured my leg to the
point that I could not move it. I had to pick my leg up with my
hands and place it back on the sled runner, and the pain was
shocking. I thought I might have to scratch at the first checkpoint. Really! After all I had gone through to get this far; I did
not want to quit after just 40 miles! I pulled into the check-

point but my team was going crazy; they didn't want to stop. I was familiar with the next section of the trail. I had run it a month earlier in another race. There were a few tricky parts but I figured I could safely get my team to the next checkpoint, 30 miles away. So I grabbed some supplies and headed out. A few hours later, I pulled into the checkpoint, parked the team, fed and bedded them down, and then lay down myself. After resting for a few hours, I felt better and decided to run to the next checkpoint. I went from checkpoint to checkpoint in this manner until, on day 10 and 630 miles into the race, my condition worsened to the point that I could no longer stand up and, for the safety of my team, I decided to scratch at the next checkpoint, the village of Kaltag.

Knowing that this was the end of my race, I went to my sled, pulled out the NORD (National Organization of Rare Disorders) banner (which I had held on the summit of Mt. Everest in 2010), limped to the front of my team, laid the banner on the ground near my dogs' feet, and snapped a picture of the banner at MY finish line. When I got back to Anchorage, I found out that my pelvis was broken in two places! I had, in fact, started the race with a broken pelvis, not just a pulled muscle. My race ended sooner than I would have liked but I had a truly amazing experience

My Finish Line with the NORD Banner, Baby Drool's feet, and my knees, March 13, 2013.

———

Before I started training for the Iditarod, Larry and I agreed that it was a two-year project. If I made it great, but if I didn't – it would be over. The time and money commitment was enormous, as was the physical and emotional stress of me living in two places. So, when I scratched at Kaltag, I knew that was the end of my sled dog racing experience, and I was fine with that. I really was. I had tried my best, gotten hurt, and had to scratch - that was that. I left Alaska and came back to my life in California and teaching at CSUF, but I missed my dogs terribly. They were never "my" dogs, but I loved and missed them so much that Larry said that we could go back to Alaska during the summer so I could give them all one last hug and say good-bye.

———

I cannot recall when or how it actually happened, but Larry said something that sparked a flame inside of me that burned to give it one more try. He said simply, "You have worked so hard, and come so far." But I thought, "no." We had agreed and Larry had been so supportive and patient with me for 5 years of my craziness that I felt that I couldn't ask for more. But he said it was up to me. Should I? Could I? Would I?

On June 29, 2013, Larry and I got out of our rental car at the Iditarod Headquarters in Wasilla, Alaska. Together we walked across the grass and over to the table. I picked up the pen, and became the fifth musher to sign up for the 2014 Iditarod. I would be running out of Vern Halter and Susan Whiton's Dream a Dream Dog Farm, and *this* time I planned on taking my NORD Banner photograph standing under the Burled Arch in Nome.

———

Just before the 2014 Iditarod Ceremonial Start. I am kissing Barge; his brother Tug is behind me, along with Kayak and Yacht.

On March 1, 2014, I started my second run at the Iditarod. Unfortunately Mother Nature made the race course unusually challenging. Of the 69 teams that started the race, 20 teams scratched, including me. I injured my shoulder coming down the Dalzell Gorge, and, for the safety of my team, I scratched at Rohn. The second chance, which I was never supposed to have, was gone. I was crushed.

Back at the kennel, Vern, an 18-time Iditarod finisher, tried to console me but to no avail. I wandered the dog yard like a disembodied soul. I just could not accept the reality of what had happened; not yet.

The next morning Larry called me. The first words I heard were, "Why don't you talk to Vern about running again next year." I could not believe my ears! I was going to get a third chance to complete the Iditarod!

————

I started my third run at the Iditarod on March 7, 2015. The trail conditions were even worse than in 2014, so the restart of the race was moved from Willow to Fairbanks. This new route took us farther north, had fewer checkpoints, and a record-breaking cold snap dropped temperatures to minus 75 degrees Fahrenheit. It was a tough race, to say the least.

On Sunday, March 22nd at 9:19 PM I crossed the Iditarod finish line in Nome. It took me 13 days, 11 hours, 19 minutes, and 51 seconds. As the final musher to complete the race, I received the Red Lantern Award, a symbol of perseverance. After extinguishing the Widow's Lantern, officially ending the race, I got my NORD banner photo standing under the Burled Arch.

Larry and I standing under the Burled Arch in Nome holding the NORD Banner.

I am the 749th individual to have completed the 1000-mile Iditarod Sled Dog Race, AND, to date, I am the only female (and 3rd person) to have both summited Mt. Everest and completed the Last Great Race! I was only 51 years old when I summited Everest and I was only 56 years old when I completed my first Iditarod Race. Too cool.

———

On May 19, 2015, I received the *Rare Disease Public Awareness Award* from the National Organization of Rare Disorders (NORD) at their *Portraits of Courage Gala* in Washington DC.

———

Alaska and the dogs have captured my heart and soul. In 2016, after 5 years of living and working in California while training and racing in Alaska, Larry and I both retired, sold our California home, bought a piece of property in Willow, and built a house. We are now Alaskans. Our house is only 6 miles from Dream a Dream Dog Farm; I just love those dogs. Did I mention that I have the most supportive and amazing husband in the world!?!

———

Addiction: On March 6, 2017, I started my fourth run at the Iditarod. Like 2015, the normal race-route was too dangerous, so once again, we started from Fairbanks.

On March 18, 2017, after 12 days, 2 hours, 57 minutes, and 31 seconds, I crossed the finish line in Nome carrying the same National Organization of Rare Disorders Banner. I received my second Red Lantern Award and set a new record for the fastest Red Lantern time in the 45-year history of the race, by more than 25 hours!

Under the Burled Arch hugging leaders Panther and Banana.

The feature-length documentary film, *Banner on the Moon*, follows Cindy Abbott, on her quest to discover the cause of her many alarming and debilitating symptoms. After 14 years, she's finally diagnosed with a rare and life-threatening disease. She sets out on an extraordinary journey to not only bring rare disease out of the darkness and into the light, but to also show how adversity can elicit hidden strength as she challenges herself to overcome one difficult feat after another... extreme endeavors of pain, perseverance, and hope.

———

I do not profess to be a spokesperson or representative for people with Wegener's granulomatosis. I am one person telling my story in an effort to bring attention and awareness to rare diseases. I know all too well how fortunate I have been, and I am very thankful. For many people with Wegener's, simple tasks such as walking their dog or getting out of bed are the mountains they climb every day.

Additionally, I have not talked about my chronic health issues because it is not my way. I do not, however, want to minimize the serious nature of this disease. Refer to the following pages for more information and resources regarding rare diseases and vasculitis.

At the National Organization for Rare Disorders (NORD), we interact with many extraordinary people. There are nearly 7,000 diseases considered rare in the United States, and together they affect almost 1 in 10 Americans. Most of these diseases are serious and lifelong. Many are life-threatening, a fact that is especially poignant because more than half of the patients are children.

However, the people affected by rare diseases - both patients and their families - tend to be unusually resourceful, hopeful, and intent upon seeking a better future for themselves and for others affected by rare diseases.

Cindy Abbott is one such person. She first contacted NORD because we are the national sponsors for Rare Disease Day in the United States. Cindy offered to work with us to help raise awareness of her own disease and also of rare diseases in general. We were thrilled with her offer, and NORD provided the Rare Disease Day banner that Cindy carried to the top of Mt. Everest. Throughout her climb, we read her blog, watched her progress, and shared her photos on our website.

NORD also works closely with the Vasculitis Foundation, one of 150 organizations that are members of NORD. We work with our member-organizations to provide advocacy, education, and other services on behalf of all people with rare diseases.

The spirit that Cindy exemplifies by her desire to educate others about her particular rare disease and her incredible determination to meet extreme challenges in spite of her disease is somehow part of *her* experience of having a rare disease. What Cindy has accomplished gives new hope to every person who has a rare disease. It reminds all of us of the importance of learning to dance in the rain.

Mary Dunkle
Vice President for Communications
National Organization for Rare Disorders (NORD)
www.rarediseases.org

Cindy Abbott is the Vasculitis Foundation's most enthusiastic spokesperson. Whether climbing the world's highest mountain or sharing her story with patients, Cindy exhibits the courage and success that we wish for all of our patients. She has unlimited energy and has shown time and time again, that a person can live life to the fullest, despite a diagnosis of vasculitis.

Cindy was diagnosed with Wegener's granulomatosis, a form of vasculitis, in 2007. Throughout her training and every day since her successful climb, Cindy has inspired and reassured patients living with vasculitis, that they too can have dreams and set goals and achieve them. As Cindy says, "Nothing is impossible." Vasculitis patients have many personal "Mt. Everest" moments in their lives and Cindy encourages them to achieve them.

The Vasculitis Foundation is the international organization for patients with vasculitis and has over 4,000 members in 58 countries. Vasculitis is a family of rare, autoimmune diseases, which affects people of all ages. Vasculitis causes inflammation of the blood vessels, arteries, veins or capillaries. There is no known cause or cure for the disease. If not treated, vasculitis can cause permanent organ damage and often death.

Receiving an early diagnosis and effective treatment is critical to patients regaining their health and avoiding serious chronic health problems. While a few of the vasculitic diseases resolve on their own, most require extensive treatment. The length of treatment varies by patient; some patients achieve remission within a year and transition to maintenance drugs while other patients use medications for years. Unfortunately, almost all vasculitis patients experience ongoing disease flares and are unable to maintain a successful remission for more than a year or two.

Prior to the 1990s, vasculitis patients lived approximately six months to two years. Now, with the advances in treatment, patients have a much brighter outlook and must learn to manage the treatment of their disease.

The Vasculitis Foundation advocates for early diagnosis, leading edge treatment and research to discover a cure for all types of vasculitis. The Foundation provides educational materials for vasculitis patients, their caregivers, family members and medical professionals. In addition, the Vasculitis Foundation provides one-on-one support for patients and their families through a network of volunteer area contacts and local chapters and support groups.

Vasculitis Foundation members and friends are encouraged to raise awareness of vasculitis and the organization year-round in their local communities. Awareness activities are directed at two constituents: the general public and the medical community. Members distribute information to medical offices/hospitals/health centers, pharmacies and libraries.

The Foundation is committed to being the world's foremost recognized resource for patients. Our goal is for patients to obtain information and education about vasculitis so that they can become their own best advocates in effectively managing and coordinating their care with their medical team. Through its website, bimonthly newsletter, information packets, 800 number and symposia the Foundation educates its members about the diseases. The educational materials provide the most current information on vasculitis, its symptoms, medications, and treatments.

The Vasculitis Foundation Research Program was established in 2001 and recently reached its initial goal to fund $1,000,000 in research. The Research Program is funded by donations, honors, memorials and special fundraising events. The Vasculitis Foundation is the largest private funder of research on vasculitis and collaborates with researchers around the world to fund the most promising studies.

Joyce A. Kullman, Executive Director
PO Box 28660, Kansas City, MO 64188-8660
816.436.8211 Phone/Fax, 800.277.9474 Toll Free
www.VasculitisFoundation.org

Gary, the owner of Press Works, has donated his graphic design services. His daughter, Holly, also has Wegener's granulomatosis.

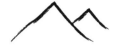

THE DOCTORS

These amazing men and women
helped diagnose, treat, stabilize, and guide me.

Dr. Gary Holland, Professor of Medicine, Division of Ophthalmology, UCLA, Jules Stein Eye Institute

Dr. Allan Kreiger, Professor of Medicine, Emeritus, Division of Ophthalmology, UCLA, Jules Stein Eye Institute

Dr. Alan Gorn, Professor of Medicine, Division of Rheumatology, UCLA, Ronald Reagan Medical Center

Dr. David Fish, Professor of Medicine, Division of Interventional Physiatry, UCLA Spine Center, Ronald Reagan Medical Center and Santa Monica Orthopedic Hospital

Dr. Peter Hackett, Director, Institute for Altitude Medicine Telluride, CO

Dr. Jonathan Ahdoot, Pulmonary Medicine and Critical Care Medicine

Dr. Jeffrey Kaufman, Urology

Dr. John Alevizos, General Medicine

Dr. Samireh Said, Dermatology and Cutaneous Oncology

Dr. Victor Strelzow, Nose and Sinus Disorders

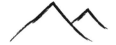

MT. EVEREST SUMMIT STATISTICS AS OF JUNE 2010

Individuals who have summited Everest ≈ 3300

Americans who have summited ≈ 430

Females who have summited Everest ≈ 260

Americans females who have summited ≈ 45

Individuals in 2010 who summited South Side of Everest by July 2010 ≈ 347

Individuals in 2010 who summited North Side of Everest by July 2010 ≈ 165

Multiple summits:

Many individuals have summited more than once. The current record is held by Apa Sherpa. On May 11, 2011, he summited Everest for the 21st time!

Accuracy:

The summit numbers are not absolute. They are a compilation using the listed sources. The intent is to give the reader a sense of how many individuals summit Mt. Everest.

Sources:

Himalayan Database, www.himalayandadtabase.com

8000ers.com, www.8000ers.com/cms

Alan Arnette, www.alanarnette.com/news

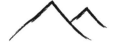

ACKNOWLEDGEMENTS

The Book
In my wildest dreams I could not have imagined that my experiences would end up in a book, and if it was not for the encouragement of my family and friends, the first word would never have been written. I must, however, express my infinite gratitude to two very special people: my husband, Larry, who stood by me every step of the way; and Stacie Parra, who made me believe it was possible.

———

The Journey
There are so many people to thank. My husband and daughter for understanding my need to follow my dream. The students, faculty, and staff at California State University, Fullerton for their support. The wonderful doctors who helped me live a better quality of life. Scott Woolums, Bill Allen, Doug Nidever, and the other individuals who taught me the skills needed to climb. Vern Halter, Lance Mackey, and Cain Carter for helping me learn how to mush. Derrick Brown, my website manager. And all the people who helped pass along my story.

ABOUT THE AUTHOR

Cindy Abbott received her master's degree in kinesiology, graduating summa cum laude from California State University, Fullerton where she taught health science and kinesiology. She was diagnosed with Wegener's Granulomatosis in 2007 and is a rare disease awareness advocate for the National Organization of Rare Disorders (NORD). As part of her advocacy, Cindy produced a feature-length documentary *Banner on the Moon*. As a key-note speaker, she continues to share her journey and her message. Cindy retired from teaching in 2016 and moved to Alaska. To date, she is the only woman to have both summited Mt. Everest and completed the 1000-mile Iditarod Sled Dog Race. Cindy travels the world searching for new adventures: climbing mountains, mushing sled dogs, and is an avid SCUBA diver and underwater videographer. A proud wife and mother, she resides in Willow, AK.

For more information go to: www.reachingbeyondtheclouds.com

Made in the USA
Columbia, SC
25 January 2022